Don't Waste Your Pretty

Your Pretty

The Go-to Guide for Making Smarter Decisions in Life & Love

Demetria L. Lucas

Books by Belle
NEW YORK, NEW YORK

Demetria L. Lucas/Books By Belle
www.ABELLEINBROOKLYN.com

Book Layout ©2013 BookDesignTemplates.com

Ordering Information:
Quantity sales. Special discounts are available on quantity purchases by corporations, associations, and others. For details, contact the "Special Sales Department" at the website above.

Don't Waste Your Pretty/ Demetria L. Lucas -- 1st ed.
ISBN 978-0-9908194-0-0 (pbk)
ISBN 978-0-9908194-1-7 (ebook)

Hi, Mom

Introduction

Confession: I became a dating coach by accident.

Let me explain.

In late 2010, I was revving up to release my first book, *A Belle in Brooklyn: The Go-to Girl for Advice on Living Your Best Single Life* (Atria). The book was based on my blog, ABelleinBrooklyn.com, where for then-four years, I had shared *some* of my dating and relationship "adventures", and those of my friends, and interviewed men about their perspective on all things women. For the book, I compiled a "best of", well, of, my experiences with men— the good, the bad, and the ugly.

I didn't write a traditional advice guide. There were no, "if you're X type of woman, do Y" tidbits laid out. I opted to tell stories since that's how I always learned best. I left it up to readers to take what they needed/wanted, or just read, and hopefully, enjoy. A friend suggested I launch a Formspring page, a site where readers could ask anonymous questions, or give me feedback or I could fill in the blanks about the book, or elaborate further. The best-case scenario was the site would operate as a sort of "Meet the Author" online book club.

What happened was much different. The early adapters wanted to know about the process of getting a book deal (hard) or writing a book (harder). Everyone else? The majority? They wanted dating and relationship advice. Though the questions and answers numbered into the thousands— 38,000 at the time of publication— we rarely discussed *A Belle in Brooklyn*.

Formspring (and the site I currently use, Ask.Fm) and its anonymity were an unseen blessing. Readers could put their business in the street without anyone knowing it was *theirs*. I realized a lot of women didn't have anyone to speak freely with about the ups and downs of like, love and/or sex. And while there were plenty of guys billing themselves as "relationship gurus" and telling women how to succeed at love, the advice often wasn't empowering, or the guys didn't always "get it" because they weren't women. Women wanted to hear from another woman. I saw a void, so I kept filling it.

I figured if I was going to help people sort through one of the most important aspects of their lives— finding and keeping love— I couldn't just wing it. To do that would make me too similar to some— not all— of the guy "gurus" I criticized. I didn't want to become one of those Internet advisers throwing witty sayings up against a picture of myself and *hoping* it made sense. I wanted to *know*. So, in the middle of prepping for the launch of *A Belle in Brooklyn*, a daunting process if ever there was one, I enrolled in life coaching school.

When I "graduated", the month before my book was published, I opened the doors to my own life coaching company, Coached By Belle. I began accepting clients and feverishly tackling all those dating and relationship questions flooding my Formspring inbox.

In the last four years, I've coached hundreds of clients and answered tens of thousands of questions on Formspring, Ask.Fm, and "Ask Belle" on ABelleinBrooklyn.com from women and men facing dating and relationship dilemmas. It didn't take long to notice some repetition in the questions: *Should I date more than one person at a time? What are the differences between girlfriend and wife "duties"? Should I give my ex a second chance? Should I tell a friend her man is cheating? How do I tell my boyfriend about my sexual assault? Can I upgrade from "friends with benefits" to girlfriend?*

I also noticed some popular patterns of behavior that led to disastrous outcomes. Many readers were investing too much time in guys (and girls) that had shown all the signs that they weren't interested; and there were a lot of good people with bad communication skills, mostly because they were afraid to ask for what they wanted. So many readers were "wasting their pretty" *and* their time *and* their affection (an overlooked commodity in the dating marketplace) *and* their energy (and sometimes money).

What you hold in your hands, or er, maybe scroll through on your e-device, is a "best of" book, because let's face it: you're not scrolling through 38,000 questions. I've complied (and categorized) the most frequent and/or popular queries I've received from real women in my coaching practice and online forums, and laid out the solutions to help you quickly jump-start your dating life, communicate better with your partner, or walk away from and get over a bad relationship. *And more.* Whatever you're going through, someone else is too, and they've probably asked me about it.

I need to give you a warning: *Don't Waste Your Pretty* isn't always pretty. I'm not an incense burning, peace and blessings, snap-instead-of-clap type of life coach. Occasionally, I will be more "Brooklyn" than I am "Belle". Sometimes I will give it to you raw. Whatever I say or how I say it, getting you into a better situation is always my goal.

Before we begin, you should also know I will challenge many of the thoughts you have about dating and relationships and friendships. Many of *us* have perspectives that aren't always beneficial to *us*. (Notice the "us". Even as a coach, I am a work in progress *too*.) I'm going to say things that may be jarring to your belief system (dating multiple people, choosing yourself first, cutting your losses quickly, etc.). I challenge you to approach *Don't Waste Your Pretty* with an open mind and I'll rise to the challenge of delivering advice that tips the dating and relationship odds in your favor.

Deal?

CHAPTER ONE

Dating 101

"Don't waste your pretty" probably doesn't mean what you think it does. Many people who've heard me use that phrase think I'm implying to women that their looks run out, and they have a limited amount of time to "make use" of that resource (i.e., snag a man). Yes and no. Looks matter. You've never seen a man across the room and thought, "ooh! I wonder how nice he is." You like the way he looks, or at minimum, how he carries himself. He notices you for the same reason you notice him, because he's *attracted.*

Your looks are what get initial attention, but they're also the least important of what you have to offer. Pretty gets you noticed, true. But it's everything else you bring to the table that gets a man interested and makes him want to come back.

"Your pretty" is a cover-all euphemism for describing your resources in the dating marketplace: your energy, emotional investment, time, listening skills, nurturing, sex, sacrifices, cheerleading, hand-holding, confidence, and more. These are resources that women often take for granted and give away to the wrong people while dating and in the *wrong* relationships. And speaking of dating— we'll get to relationships down the line (page 69)— let's get into some reader questions about how to get a date:

"Some people suggest you stop looking, focus on other things and eventually a man will find you. What do you think?"

I've never understood this concept. For everything you've ever achieved in life— your diploma/degree, your promotion, the money you saved to buy that must-have stiletto— you were willing to put in the effort to have it. Finding a partner is no different. You probably spent your hard-earned money on this book because you're frustrated and you want a partner *now*. And if you want someone and you don't want to gamble for it to "eventually" happen, you have to go after it. *Now.*

That doesn't mean you start hunting men down like you would a new dress for an event where your Ex and his Next will be present. It does mean you do what I call a "cutie run". That means when you see a man you might be interested in, you smile, instead of looking away like most of us were trained to do so as not to appear "fast". Your goal is to be noticed, and appear friendly and approachable.

Smiling women are profoundly rare so that's usually all it takes for a man to come over and chat enthusiastically. I figured this out when I was 27. It's only *not* worked for me once, and later I found out it wasn't personal. The guy who looked at me blankly? A professional athlete who was publicly dragged out of the closet by his alleged boyfriend years later.

If you see someone cute and you haven't caught his eye yet, walk up and ask him a question or pay him a compliment. For many years my "line" was "Hi, [smile]. I like your shirt." Or "Excuse me, [smile] where did you get your shirt from?" You can literally say or ask anything. Guys are pretty simple. All they see is a smiling, attractive woman in their face. If he's remotely interested, he will pick up the conversation from there. Men have been practicing how to talk to women since they were tweens.

"I've been single for almost two years, and I don't want to be. I've been dating; some guys were nice enough but we just didn't click, but most weren't up to par or didn't want to be in

a relationship. I'm tired of being the single one, of dating and all the games, and it never goes anywhere. Is it me? Should I move?"

Since 2011, I've been on a perpetual book tour in multiple cities, including Washington, D.C., Atlanta, Chicago, Houston, Dallas, Philadelphia, Boston, New Orleans, Los Angeles, and Johannesburg. In each city, I encounter women who lament the dating options where they are as the worst like, ever, and many wonder if they'd have better luck somewhere else. I've yet to come across any bunch of women in any city, in the U.S. or abroad, who say, "Yes, I have more options of suitable, relationship-minded partners than I know what to do with." So if you like mostly everything about your city except the dating options, stay put and make do with what you have.

If it makes you feel the tiniest bit better: You are far from alone, when it comes to being "the single one." A recent Pew Research Center study found that 49 percent of American adults are single.

Finding a partner is supposed to be hard. For any other less monumental decision, like picking the right car or renting an apartment or deciding on a college, there is a frustrating process to go through before you make the right choice. Dating is no different.

"Gave a guy friend a few compliments and he replied, "you do have a soft side!" He told me that he knows I'm nice, but most guys only see the educated, successful, 'don't take no mess' me. This isn't the first time I've heard this. What can I do to look more approachable?"

This is going to sound trite, but it works: smile. And pay compliments. As soon as you did it, your guy friend began to see you in a different, more desirable light. So do it more often.

Educated and successful aren't the problem. The kind of man you want, wants a woman who's doing things and going places. It's the "don't take no mess" look that's scaring men away. It's a necessary persona that many women have to adopt to get through the day and of course, there are times that are "just one of them days that a girl goes through." But if you're trying to catch the interest of the opposite sex, the tough-girl façade reads as "not interested", "doesn't want to be bothered", and worse, "will reject me." If you want to be approached, you've got to look like a guy has a shot.

"I was always good at throwing a smile and starting conversations. But I backed off doing that because friends say it doesn't allow the man to pursue me first. What do you think about that?"

I think you're friends are probably jealous of your confidence with men and the attention you get from them. And by listening to them, you're blocking your blessings. Smiling and starting a conversation is getting noticed, which if you're single and don't want to be, is your goal. You were doing well. Go back to that.

That said, I'm not a fan of asking a man for his number, calling first, or asking him out first. It works for some women, but if you're like me, you want to know for sure that a man is interested and you need to see him put in some work like taking the initiative to get in contact again.

"Exactly where should I go for a cutie run? You've said clubs/bars are bad places to meet men. Why? What about lounges?"

Anywhere. Literally.

Somehow we all got this idea that we have to go to places where there are likely to be groups of men. And we go to these places looking and even if we find them, what do we also find? Groups of women, lots of groups, and the ratio of women to men is 10:1.

You will meet more men just going through your daily life than you ever will in any club or bar, and you won't have to yell over the music. Daily life means at the gas station, waiting in line at the dry cleaner, walking though CVS, running an errand on your lunch break, etc. There are men everywhere. You just have to pay attention... and smile.

To specifically answer your questions about clubs and bars: good people go to them all the time. The person you meet is a slightly altered version of himself just like you. "Club You" isn't typically day-to-day you. The reason you go to the club is to turn-up from your usual self. And "Bar You" is tipsy, at least. Neither you nor the person you've met really know what they're getting until you meet up sober, if you remember each other. Lounges are a better option. People tend to be more mellow there than the club.

"I'm recently divorced after 12 years of marriage. When out on a cutie run and someone asks for my number, should I hand them my business card or tell them to get their phone out so that he/I can type it in? How do people do it these days?"

Don't do the business card, too impersonal and implies you want to do work. Put your number in his phone or dictate it to him. If he is interested, he will call.

"I'm Facebook friends with my brother's friend of 15+ years. I find him attractive from his pics and thoughts. Met two weeks ago and exchanged 'it was great meeting you' messages the day after. How do I make a Facebook cutie run?"

Like his posts and comment, then follow up with a direct message to have a conversation one-on-one. After a few exchanges, he should holler if he's interested.

Or not. You being his boy's brother may give him pause. The men may need to chat before he steps to you. And you may need to be more direct to make it clear that you're interested. If after the third private message he's not asking for your number or to see you, let him know you would like to see him again.

"I went to a networking event with a friend and there were a lot of men present. She was attached to my hip the whole night. I'm not a social butterfly, but I'm making attempts to meet men. I had to keep making excuses to get away from her to approach people. Friend said I left her. Was I wrong?"

Not wrong, per se. You just didn't communicate your expectations. She's used to ya'll going out and sticking together. You've got a new strategy and switched up, but didn't tell her. Apologize for "abandoning" her to keep the peace, then explain your intentions. This should patch things up quickly.

Also, the new approach is good. Men feel more comfortable one-on-one than trying to holler at you *and* an audience *and* entertaining your friend at the same time.

"Not into playing games, but is it true that guys notice women who aren't as "pressed" more than they do the opposite? I really like this guy but I've noticed women throw themselves at him. I definitely show interest, but usually take a more reserved approach and let him come to me. Right or wrong?"

Depends on the guy.

Funny, a lot of what women call being "thirsty" or "pressed" is basic flirting. Women have asked questions about whether striking up a conversation is "pressed" or paying a compliment is "thirsty" (see the previous question about the friends who were mad about smiling). Many of us believe showing any interest in the opposite sex is doing too much. But looking interested actually makes you look friendly and approachable and more likely to meet someone.

In general, what women tend to think of as "reserved" is next to doing nothing from a guy's perspective. Men don't do hints well. You don't have to throw yourself on anyone, but do smile, and flirt, which loosely means touch him— an arm is fine— keep your upper body turned toward him, look interested when he speaks and smile *a lot.*

"Do you think people should be set up on blind dates? How do you feel about them?"

Sure. Why not? If you are single and don't want to be, you should use every available, safe, and moral option to meet people.

Several years ago, I allowed my mother, my boss, and my best friend to each pick a person for me to go on a blind date with and I wrote about the adventure for *Essence* Magazine. A couple tips based on that experience:

Moms pick nice (but kind of boring) guys who are looking to nest. The guy my mother picked was several years older than me and got married less than a year after we met.

Your single best friend will pick someone cute and fun, but without long-term potential (which is fine. Every date is not supposed to be your man or your husband.) Your married friend may choose better.

Your boss (or co-worker) will pick a better mate than the two people who should know you better than anyone else. I didn't have a love connection with my boss's pick, but we did have a second date and we're still friends almost five years later.

DATING OUT

"I'm proud to be single and loving it, though I must admit having a companion is inviting. The dating scene can be so brutal and non-rewarding when measuring quality over quan-

tity. When is the right time to date outside of your race?"

Right now! Today! This very moment!

If you want a companion, your goal should be to find a partner who gets you and treats you well, *period*. And there are people of all colors who are capable of doing that.

You're right. Quality is what matters most, and there are potential partners of quality in every race. Don't limit yourself to one race just to say you did, or out of blind allegiance. You're cutting yourself off from meeting a potentially good mate.

A couple things to note about dating "out":

Dating outside your race isn't a back up plan for not being able to find a match with someone of the same race. Every race of people has its crazies, its lazies, its liars and its cheats. You will still encounter foolish and non-genuine people no matter what color they are or which culture they come from.

Continue to date men who share your race. You don't have to cut off one group in order to explore other options. The goal is to find the right person for you. That could be a person of your own race— or not.

Don't limit your dating "out" options solely to white men. Black women tend to think that "dating out" means "dating white." There are more options than that, and they come with melanin.

"Even though I am a Black woman, does that mean I should only limit myself to Black men? Would you ever date outside your race?"

I went to a predominately white high school and two predominately white colleges. I usually gravitated to the Black guys, but there are two exceptions. In high school, I briefly dated a white boy. He kind of looked like "Zack Morris" from *Saved by the Bell*. I think it was the haircut.

Anyway, he had never dated a Black girl before. I had never dated a white boy. Once we got over the (ignorant) misconceptions we each had about what white people liked and what Black people did, we started interacting like *just people* and it was fine. He was a good listener and as a music-head, he introduced me to artists I never heard of and liked. Race wasn't really a factor, or maybe we didn't date long enough for it to become one.

In college, I met a guy outside a party, whose parents were Egyptian, and we dated for a few months. He was a first-generation American who was raised in a Black neighborhood and when I met him, he was training to be a teacher at an HBCU. Nice guy. We're friends on Facebook.

I respect the perspective of Black women who only want to date Black men. I get it. But I see no reason for Black women who are interested in nonblack men to "limit" themselves as some act of race-loyalty, especially when Black men don't always return "the favor" *while dating* (88 percent of Black men marry Black women, according to researchers Ivory A. Toldson of Howard University and Bryant Marks of Morehouse College). For various reasons, straight guys are interested in women they find attractive and her particular hue matters way less.

"As an African-American woman, I find it difficult to date. Most of my family discourages me from dating outside my race, but I haven't really met any African-American men who I get along with. Is it me"?

Your family doesn't have to date them, *you do*. But since they are so involved in your dating life, tell your concerned family to put some so-called "skin in the game" and hook you up with Black *men*— plural, you need options— that would be a good match. In the meantime, date nice men of any color that you are attracted to and who treat you well *and* don't tell your family. They can only comment on what they know about.

"When guys from other races approach me or seem to express interest, I feel like I am their cultural project and quickly shut it down. They don't say anything offensive, but I wonder why they want a Sista when they have not

ventured over to this side before— or seem to have not to. Is this odd?"

Odd implies that it's out of the ordinary, but I've heard this reaction from some Black women toward non-Black men several times.

To be fair, there are non-Black men who hold weird beliefs about Black women. You didn't just pull that idea from the sky. But you're being unfair to assume every non-Black guy's outlook on Black women is some sort of "Venus Hottentot" fetish. There are other ways of looking at this scenario. Other Black women that will hear a non-Black guy is interested and think, *of course he is. Why wouldn't he be? Black is beautiful,* and they would entertain the guy (and be right).

Some Black women cannot fathom this. We've heard from so many sources— including some Black men— that there is something wrong with Black women, that Black women aren't worthy of respect, or there's only one "type" of Black woman that is. Because of that, sometimes we can't wrap our heads around anyone else wanting us. It's unfortunate that some folks have bought into the negative hype.

The next time you're approached by a man of any color who is attractive, interesting, and respectful, give him a chance to show you what he's about instead assuming the worst and "quickly" shutting him down.

"A guy contacted me on a dating site and started off with 'I don't normally date outside my race or my comfort zone, but you're beautiful and caught my eye.' I feel a certain way about that statement. I want someone who will be comfy with dating a Black woman. Am I reading too much into it?"

Many single women have been brainwashed into thinking that everyone deserves a shot, lest a woman find herself single forever because she wasn't open-minded. To be clear, you're not obligated to accept his offer just to have a date. You're single, not desperate. The two are not synonymous.

You can turn this guy down or flat-out ignore his interest and not doom your chances of meeting someone. There are plenty of Black and non-Black men who desire to date a Black woman, have dated one before and are more than comfortable doing so. They can also string together an opening line that won't offend you.

ONLINE DATING

"I'm in a new city and it's a little tough to meet quality men. I know they're out there but they're just not crossing my path. Is 23 too young to start looking for love online?"

"Looking for love" or just a date online is not an act of desperation. Forty million Americans use online dating services, according to Match.com. That's about 40 percent of the country's single population.

Online dating sites are a convenient way to help you meet people that you might not "encounter" in your day-to-day travels or within your social circle. The bonus is you can meet men in your pajamas and scarf, and without leaving your living room.

That said, dating sites are not the only tool that you should be using. You should be operating on all cylinders to meet potential mates. Continue to go out and make yourself available to meet people, ask friends and family who they know that might be a good match, *and* look online.

"Dating online. He contacted me first, and I'm not sure how to proceed. Should I be doing the calling and contacting or let him go forward?"

The rules of dating don't change just because you meet online. He's done the real world equivalent of crossing a room to say, "hello". Proceed the same way you would if you met him while you were out by responding in a way that conveys your degree of interest.

If you're interested, respond with a note that mirrors his in tone, detail and length. After two to three exchanges, if you like what you're reading, take the conversation off-line. Suggest that he call you and/or you Skype/FaceTime/Tango. If he's interested, he will call or set up a time to video chat with you.

Don't get stuck here. Online dating is a place where you meet people, but not the place where you *date* them. After a week, two tops for the most hesitant online daters, if he doesn't suggest you actually meet, then you suggest it. If he can't meet, you can't date him. You will not set yourself up to be catfish-ed.

"Been talking to a guy I met online over a year ago. Lately, we only talk through text. He's invited me to visit though. Does this mean he's interested?"

Interested men pick up the phone. The invite sounds like an ask just to see what you'll say. If you make your way out to visit him, expect drama.

Be wary of guys who do all or most of their communicating via text. Texting is what people do when they are busy doing something else and are bored. And also when they can't pick up the phone, usually because they don't want someone nearby to overhear the conversation. It sounds like your guy has lost interest in you and found it in someone else. But he'll catch if you opt to throw yourself at him.

"First date with a guy and he says my dating profile makes me sound angry. My profile literally says, "I learned a lot from past relationships and based on that, I want to be with someone genuine, isn't full of drama, smart

and fun." How is that angry? And if he felt that way, why ask me out?"

Eh... he probably asked because he thinks you're attractive and wants to have sex with you, and maybe because he wants to judge in person whether you're angry or not. If he genuinely thinks you're angry after meeting you, he's not going to pursue anything serious.

So about your profile... I wouldn't say it's angry, as much as it practically screams, "I've been sh---ed on and I'm not over it!" The first thing you list is about past relationships, which though most of us have, no one wants to hear about upfront. Then you follow that by listing the basics— drama-fee, genuine, as if these traits have been unattainable in the aforementioned past relationships. It sounds like you're not accustomed to good treatment. Women who have been treated poorly often have a chip on their shoulder. That's probably why he summed you up as angry.

Let's clean up your profile. Remove the mention of past relationships, and don't bring it up until after the third face-to-face date unless he specifically asks. (Feel free to pry into his past if he does.) List traits that give more insight into your hobbies/interests and make you sound interesting, for instance, loves to travel, likes roller coasters, antique aficionado, etc.

"Should you limit yourself to dating locally (less than an hour drive) when it comes to online dating?"

Yes. Long distance relationships work best when you and your partner date in the same town/city and establish a connection first, and then one person moves away for whatever reason. It's very hard to build *and maintain* a connection when there's a large distance. The travel begins to wear and tear on even the most dedicated of couples. (I know from personal experience.)

"Been calling and Skype-ing with a dude I met on a dating site. Met a few times while he was in my area on business trips. Now he wants to visit *me* in my city. Should I offer to pay for his airfare? (He hasn't asked. Just curious.)"

Men respect what they work for. And you are worth the effort and expense. Let that working man come to you. Show your appreciation by offering to pick up a tab *once* during his visit.

"I've been getting to know this guy I met online three months ago. I was in his city for a friend's birthday and we made plans to meet up. He kept making excuses that he was running late and eventually "fell asleep." I want to believe him, but I can't. Should I?"

No. He was probably with his girlfriend, or at the very least, another woman. What's for sure is he didn't want to see you, otherwise he would have.

Keep it 300: you went to his city *partially* because your friend was having a party, and *partially* because you wanted to meet him. You made yourself convenient and he still dropped the ball.

His excuses don't even make sense. People who are running late eventually show up. And if they are so late that they no longer see a point in coming, they text or call to say, "hey, I'm not going to make it. How can I see you before you leave?"

Once when I was living in Maryland, I went to New York for the day for a job interview. I called a guy I had been dating in the city to let him know I'd be in town. He told me he had a meeting and wouldn't be able to steal away to see me. I understood, but I was terribly disappointed.

While I was in the city a few days later, he called to ask my schedule and I shared that I was on the 7PM train home. He called me at 6:45. I assumed he felt bad and was making sure I made it to my train on time. Instead, when I answered, he told me to meet him under the clock in Penn Station. We hung out for 15 minutes.

He wanted to see me. It was inconvenient. He made it happen, even briefly. Your guy could too. He didn't.

Take this for the big, bright flashing red stop sign that it is, and stop dating him.

FIRST ENCOUNTERS

"How important are sparks when you meet someone?"

Meh. Not very. It feels good to go gaga over someone, but that feeling doesn't last *consistently* even when you're really attracted and interested. You also can't guarantee anything that matters— good treatment, communication, consistent interest, etc.— off of sparks.

Sparks are hard to come by— but so the newbie daters know, they can happen with more than one person— so when you find them, entertain at least a date. But if you're not getting what you need *in addition* to sparks, cut ties. Also, don't rule a great guy out because he doesn't make you want to wall-slide at "hello". Sparks are a thing, but not *everything* or anything important.

"How do you stay grounded when you first meet a man you vibe with? Sometimes it's easy to think about the 'what ifs' and 'maybe he could be serious'. I usually let him show me with his actions and end up disappointed. How do you zero your expectations?"

It's easy to think, fantasize really, about a guy you don't know. He's a blank slate that you can project anything on to. But you're not doing yourself or him any favors when that happens. You're creating a image in your head of who he is, and one that's nearly impossible to live up to. Even the greatest guy is imperfect.

The solution isn't to "zero your expectations", but to stop fantasizing and let the guy show you who he is— flaws and all— and judge whether that works for you or not.

"When you meet a guy, should you tell him upfront, like first convo, what it is that you are looking for, i.e., serious relationship with marriage potential, or should you see where it goes first?"

See where it goes. Asking that question upfront reads as, "I'm not interested in *you*. I just want to be in a relationship with or married to *anyone.*"

Even if you asked that question upfront and he said "yes!" with enthusiasm, if you're not a good fit for him, what difference would it make? He wouldn't be committing *to you.* Actually get to know him, and evaluate him to see if he's compatible with you.

"I agree with Steve Harvey, who says if you tell a guy that you like flowers and candy, he will buy that until he gets what he wants.

When you tell a new guy what you like and what you want, isn't that basically giving him a "road map to your heart?"

If it all it takes is flowers and candy to capture your heart or get in your panties, then you need a more intricate map and higher standards.

Men are not mind readers. If you don't tell a man what you like and want, you're not likely to get it. It's like expecting your boss to give you a promotion without ever asking for one. I mean it happens sometimes, but usually long after you thought you deserved it.

You want a good potential partner? Tell them what you want and what you expect, then watch their words and actions for consistency *over time*. It's easy to make grand gestures, and significantly harder to fake day-to-day interest.

"Been out several times with a guy. He's paid every time (pretty expensive). He's also cooked for me once. He's jokingly mentioned that he would like to be taken out/ wined and dined. I don't know how I feel about this. What's your take on paying for dates?"

You should get on board and either pick up the tab for the next date or throw down in the kitchen for him sometime soon, *if* you want to continue dating him.

Right now, you're not being an active participant in the dating process. (Showing up and looking pretty isn't enough). From his perspective, you seem selfish. You're more than willing to accept his generosity, but at the mere suggestion that you do for him what he has done for you on multiple occasions, you balk.

"I went on a date and offered to pay the tip. Guy got upset and said I was trying to upstage his manhood. How do I correct things?"

Oh, he's one of those. That's not chivalry, it's hyper-masculinity compensating for a massive insecurity. Unless you're a really "traditional" woman, this won't work in the long run. He has rigid (i.e., stifling) beliefs about the roles for men and women and he will expect you to abide by them religiously. Dinner isn't the only place where this outlook shows up.

"I met a guy who told me that the moment he saw me, he knew I was 'the One.' He asked for permission to court me and then started saying he was my man. I found out that he went on a date and he's been telling the other woman he's interested in her, too. I told him, 'I'm done.' He says I'm overreacting, he's single and not committed and he can take out whomever he wants. My issue was what he was saying to me *and her*. Was I wrong?"

It's frustrating to emotionally invest in someone, buy into his or her words and then discover that what you thought was the situation, actually wasn't. He's culpable for selling you a dream, even if doing so is a widely practiced and culturally accepted method of dating. This notion dictates that a man can say or do whatever works to win a woman's affection— emotional and physical— and that it's up to the woman to decipher his true intentions.

For intentionally misleading you to believe that he was more serious than he was, he was wrong. For dating someone else? Not so much. He's single, and, like he said, he can do as he pleases with whomever he pleases. *So can you.*

Unless there's a commitment or a conversation specifically about not dating anyone else— implying it doesn't count— you should assume that the person you're interested in is seeing, and likely having sex with, at least one other person. It doesn't mean he's not interested in you— just that he has multiple interests. That's pretty much what dating is these days.

The drama in this situation isn't all on him, though. You weren't wrong, but you were extraordinarily naive. The idea of spotting you across the room and knowing immediately that you are his destiny is the stuff of fairytales and old-school R&B lyrics, *not reality*. And while every woman should be confident enough to think she's worthy of inspiring such feelings, she should also be *realistic* enough to accept that those feelings come, not off of an initial glance, but over time.

The second sign he wasn't what he seemed was when he started calling himself your man. There's an element of dysfunctional romance to it. It's just odd for a guy to declare himself your man and not give you a say. That's not how commitments are established. At the very least, there is— or there should be— a discussion about what's going on between the two of you and what to expect from a relationship.

He was spitting game. It pains me to write my next sentence, because it's so pessimistic, but it's also real: *You cannot trust that every man who says he's all about you actually is.* Men should not mislead women about their intentions (and for clarity, women should not mislead men). But until people *en masse* stop doing it, the onus will always be on you to decipher the games, the lines and the lies in order to protect yourself.

If you're seeking a healthy relationship, take *months* slowly getting to know someone— i.e., dating. There's a reason it's called *building* a relationship.

"I told a male friend that I'm tried of falling for liars, and from now on, I'm going to make potentials answer my interview questionnaire. I showed him my questions and he said it's the silliest thing he's ever seen. I think it's brilliant and it's accountability. People lie in the beginning and down the line they do the opposite of what they told you. With my paper, it's written proof. What do you think?"

While I get what you're trying to do in theory, no, just no. Do you think that the guys who lie care if they put it on paper? People lie to themselves, and as Lauryn Hill once observed, "lie to *God* too, so what makes you think they won't lie to you?"

The best way to protect your heart is to take your time getting to know folks, let the consistency of their actions *over time* show you that they are able to be trusted, and then keep both eyes open. A questionnaire won't save you from heartache, and equally important, when you break it out, it will drive sane men away.

THE EARLY STAGES

"When I'm dating a guy, I often ask him what he's looking for. More times than not, his response is something like, "I honestly don't know." When I hear that, I assume red flag and that they want sex and don't want to say it. Am I right?"

It's not the red flag you think it is. There are a couple issues going on here. One of them is that guys don't know all the answers. Sometimes we act like they are supposed to.

That's a hard question for most guys and most people, even "good" ones, to answer. It's like a potential employer saying, "so tell me about yourself" in an interview. There's a lot to tell, you don't know exactly what the person wants to know, you don't know where to begin, you don't want to turn them off and so, your brain goes blank. The other issue is that only women are told to make lists of what they're looking for. It's just not a directive given to guys.

The "honestly, I don't know" is more than likely genuine. He showed up for a date hoping to spend time with a pretty woman, but he's getting hit with level 10 questions out of the blue, and can't come up with a cohesive, un-jumbled response on the spot.

Don't write him off because he doesn't have an answer ready. Tell him you would like him to think about it and let you know his thoughts after he's had some time to mull it over. If he's interested, he'll get back to you. It's not a big ask. Also, if a man is remotely attracted to you, he wants sex. It doesn't make him undateable unless that's *all* he wants.

"When meeting/dating guys, I'm always fighting some conspiracy theory. It's like I always have to be on high alert. Dating seems like such a chore. When can one just relax?"

Now. Right now! As long as you're on "high alert" and suspicious of everything, you're no fun to be around.

I know why you do it: it's a protection mechanism to stop yourself from being disappointed or deceived. But when you walk around looking for the bad in everyone— which everyone has— you're going to find it and miss the good.

You want to protect yourself? Be easy, have fun and *go slow* getting to know people. That means take your time before you invest your heart, ask a lot of questions, listen to the answers, and observe whether *actions* and words match consistently *over time*. (I keep repeating this for a reason. I want it to sink in.)

"When dating, I don't want to be too available, so sometimes I don't answer calls. I don't go missing for hours, but I believe I don't have to be at his attention constantly. My friend says I'm playing games. I say, 'it's OK.'"

Your friend is right. I agree with you on not needing to be available all the time, but you need to actually be busy, not pretending to be unavailable and doing nothing. The "games" are in the pretending.

Don't be pseudo-busy, actually have something interesting to do. There's nothing worse than the person you can't get on the phone and when you finally do,

they have nothing to talk about because they're not
doing anything.

**"How important is 'the chase' to guys? Do
they want to do it? Where's the line between
being hard to get versus being easy?"**

The chase is everything, and the laziest man alive
will happily do it for a woman he is interested in. One
of the reasons I'm not such a fan of women asking guys
for their numbers, or asking them out, is because many
men just don't respect a woman *in the long-run* when
she does the heavy-lifting upfront. Women chasing is
fun and it strokes the ego, but guys respect what they
work for, and they tend to treat you better when they
feel like they had to put in effort for your interest.

If you've ever been around a married man telling his
version of the "how I met my wife" story, the gist of it
is *always* some version of "I saw this fine woman, came
correct, jumped through some hoops, convinced her to
marry me and she did." It's entirely sexist— not liking
the perspective, doesn't stop it from being the way
guys think— but men tend to think of women as a reward for hard work.

**"How do you feel about situations where a lot
of women are interested in the same guy?
What if there is someone you think is really
cool, but you know a lot of other women are**

interested in him as well? Do you proceed or just forget it?"

Proceed. You don't want someone that no one else wants. It means there's a great flaw that you're overlooking.

If a lot of people like him, don't fall into the trap of trying to prove you're better than the other women interested in him. He won't respect it. Be your best you. If he's interested, he'll *act* like it and not try to put you in competition with other women.

"I have two *great* guys I've known for a while who are into me, but I'm not feeling either of them. I just feel guilty that I don't want to give them a chance when they are such great men. I just don't like them the way I feel I should for a relationship. What to do?"

If these were men you recently met and didn't know well, I'd say give them at least a couple of dates to get to know them better, since sometimes it takes a few encounters to build chemistry or interest. Not every guy is an expert at wooing women, and some need a little time to get over their jitters— yes, men have them, too. But you've known these guys and you're still yawning. Let them know that you appreciate their interest, but don't feel the same. Tell them this as soon as possible so they don't feel misled.

About your guilt: there's no reason to feel that way. Only you can determine who is the right person and what is the right feeling to have about him. As a single woman, even one who may want to be in a relationship, there is nothing wrong with refusing to settle.

You have been fortunate enough to attract the interest of two "great" men. Have faith that you can attract a few more and that one of them will be not "just" a good guy, but the *right* guy.

"How do you feel about people who are newly dating going 'Dutch' for a couple of months? I hear some men saying if a woman wants to hold out for 90 days before sex, then they're holding out on buying (paying for dinner, movies, etc.) for the same length of time. What say you?"

He doesn't really like you if he's not willing to pay for a couple of dinners here and there. You offer to pay every 3-4 dates to show you are also interested and willing to financially invest in getting to know him.

The logic expressed here is putting a price tag on sex. The 90-day rule isn't about seeing how much a man will spend on you before sex (or it's not supposed to be). It's about actually getting to know a man before figuring out if you want to share a very intimate experience with him. The guy that feels like he's buying sex with dinner and/or a movie isn't the guy you want to date anyway. And unfortunately, there are lot of men who think this way.

EXCLUSIVITY

"What is the difference between dating and being in a relationship?"

Dating is an activity. "In a relationship" is an actual, well, relationship status.

Many women weren't taught how to date. We meet a guy, and as soon as our number is entered in his phone, we go from 0 to 100 real quick. We meet him, and we cut off all other potential options to "see where it goes." That's not dating. It is hustling backwards.

There's no commitment in dating. But many dating women may feel like they are in a relationship because they've focused all their attention on one man. If you're ever in doubt about whether you're dating or in a relationship, recall the conversation you had with him about commitment. If you didn't have one, you're dating. And he shouldn't be your only option.

"I'm not in a committed relationship, but I am dating someone (nothing physical). Another guy asked me on a date, which I accepted. My friends are giving me grief, saying I should date one person at a time and give it a chance to grow. Am I wrong?"

Your friends are good people, who are giving bad advice. Exclusivity is for committed relationships, and since you aren't in one, you shouldn't act like you are. If the guy you're dating doesn't want you to see other people, then he should offer you a commitment and a title. And so you know, if he hasn't asked you to be in a relationship, he's not exclusive to you. (And he shouldn't be. He's single.)

Here's the thing, what if you only date this first guy for months, finally ask him, "Where is this going?" and he hits you back with "I like things the way they are" or "I just want to be friends." You're stuck starting over from scratch after months invested and no commitment to show for it. That's a waste of your pretty.

Exclusivity is also a resource. One of the many reasons men commit, other than "just" liking you, is because they see you have a lot to offer, know other men will notice and they don't want you entertaining other men. If he's got the core bonuses of a relationship without actually being in one, there's no incentive to commit.

"Is it unfair to date someone when you have no plans of committing to them?"

Sometimes you just want some good company and there is nothing wrong with that. If you sense that the other person is looking to move forward with you, then you should be honest about your lack of interest. If the

guy wants to continue to date despite your unwilling-
ness for it to "go somewhere", you're in the clear. However, things do tend to get messy when one person is
more interested than the other, and you are best served
in the long run to move on.

**"When you're dating different guys and the
convo comes up about who you are seeing,
should you let the guy know that he's not the
only one? And how many are too many too
date?"**

Be honest, but vague. He doesn't need a run down
of when you went out, where you went, or what happened with who. But if he wants to know if he's the
only person you're seeing, tell him, "I am dating and
exploring my options right now." If he wants you to
date him exclusively, suggest that he offer a commitment. You're a one-man woman *when you're in a relationship.*

If he presses for details, your answer is a polite,
"I'm really just not comfortable sharing that with you."
And smile.

Oh, and date as many people as you are interested
in. There's no cut off number.

**"How can a man ever feel a deeper connection
or know that he wants to take it to the next**

level with someone if he's dividing his time between multiple women?"

The purpose of dating, other than having fun, is to figure out who you like or don't. You build a deep connection via communication. That "he gets me!" feeling that you have when you meet a special guy? You don't need to be exclusive to explore that. Your "deep connections" are built in relationships, not dating. You should require the security of being "us against the world" to really get deep.

"How should I handle a situation where I see a guy I'm dating out with another woman? Speak to both parties? Speak only to the guy? Don't speak?"

Speak politely in your friendliest voice to him, then to her. Don't show any affection. Add that it was good seeing him. Then walk away. If you can't manage to be a mature adult, avoid speaking and just keep it moving.

"A part of dating is kissing, sex, and stuff. How does that work when I'm dating multiple people?"

I advocate for the old school rule, which is you don't have concurrent sex partners, and you definitely do not have sex with more than one person in the same menstruation cycle. I don't say that for moral reasons, more like practical and health.

Concurrent sexual partners puts you at a higher risk for sexually transmitted infections. It also makes things super tricky if you get pregnant. You never want to find yourself in the position of a *Maury* guest, guessing whom you're pregnant for.

You can kiss anyone you want, though you're certainly not obligated to because you went on a date— or several.

"If you're dating someone that you really like— but not exclusively— it's okay to sleep with other people to keep the hormones in check, right?"

If you're not in a relationship, you can do what you want, and you don't have to be accountable to anyone but yourself.

It's your body and you can do what you want with it. I only ask that whoever you choose to sleep with, you both get tested for sexually transmitted infections, including HIV, and use condoms consistently. And you should be honest about your current sex life with all of your sexual partners.

Oh, and you can keep your hormones in check by masturbating. It's gets you off, you don't have to get tested first and you don't need a partner.

"Do you have any advice for those that find it hard to date multiple people? I've tried and I

honestly don't enjoy it. It's nearly impossible for me to like two or more guys at once and part of me feels guilty for wasting a guy's time if I'm not really feeling him."

You know what I don't enjoy? Working out. I do it as a means to an end so I can always find dresses that I want in my size. Dating multiples might be your version of me going to the gym. I can't suggest to you in good conscience that you waste your resources on unproven men and make choices that ultimately don't benefit you just because you don't like them. Putting all your eggs in one clichéd basket is a gamble that you don't need to take.

I wouldn't suggest that you continue to date a guy who you're completely not interested in and/or not having fun with. I will suggest that even after you meet a man that you like, that you continue to give a shot to other men who interest you. If one of the guys you are seeing has an issue with you dating multiples, he'll ask you to commit. Don't give your leverage away.

CHAPTER TWO

Miss Independent

There's a "type" of woman that tends to be drawn to my style of advice. She's got something going on for herself, she has an education (or is getting one current-ly) and high expectations, and while she wants a part-ner, she's not going to wait to have one to live the fabulous grown-up life she imagined as a girl. Because of her ambition and accomplishments, she's been told that it will be hard for her to find a mate.

I've heard this concern from students who worry that by majoring in math or engineering or computer science that they will be perceived as "too smart." I've heard it from corporate women who are intentionally vague about what they do for a living so as not to be in competition with or scare off a potential mate. I've read about this phenomenon countless times in any of those 50-11 articles that point out the death of marriage and always blame feminism, women with degrees and women in the workforce as the culprits. I've done it, downplaying my job as "just a writer" when I met my now-fiance, CBW, because I thought author-editor-columnist-award-winning blogger would be too much for him to handle. (It wasn't.)

Here's what I wish I knew then, and what you should know now: the more educated you are, the more likely you are to get married. And not only get married, but *stay* married, according to a recent study by professors at Howard University and Morehouse College. The study took a look at ladies in Atlanta—and you've heard how hard it is to date there— and found that 67 percent of women with a doctoral degree were married, and 55 percent of women with a master's degree had tied the knot. The study reported Black women in Washington, D.C. had similar marriage rates. If you need more optimism, the same study found that by age 35, 75 percent of Black women have headed down the aisle at least once. Among Black women, 70 percent of Black female college graduates are married by 40, according to a briefing paper from the Council on Contemporary Families.

"Entrepreneurial elements of America have found a variety of creative ways to benefit financially from black females' anxieties at the expense of black males' egos," say the authors of the study, Ivory A. Toldson, Ph.D., an associate professor at Howard University School of Education, and Bryant T. Marks, an assistant professor of psychology at Morehouse College. "Preachers, entertainers turned relationship experts, filmmakers and news documentaries have manipulated statistics to stoke the fear necessary to sell their pre-ferred cut-rate brand of catharsis or solace." In other words, don't believe the hype.

Smart men— the only kind you want as a part-ner— know the advantage of having a power player by their side. In 2012, I spoke about dating and relation-ships to a ladies-only room at the National Black Law Students Association. After the panel, I struck up a conversation with a man in the lobby, also a lawyer, who was newly married and happily bragging about his wife's professional successes. He told me he had been the breadwinner in their relationship until she opened a catering business that was currently baking dough and raking it in. Thinking back to the panel, I asked him, "Are you bothered by her success?"

He didn't let me down. "Hell, no!" he exclaimed in a thick Southern accent. "When she's winning, I'm win-ning!" Lucky for you, I've encountered many, many men who think like he does.

Check out these successful women who are trying to manage dating and relationships:

"I'm tired of being alone, but I work long hours. How do you balance work and relationships?"

You make time. Just like you worked to get your degree(s) and job and promotion(s), you have to put in the same effort to have a relationship. It doesn't just happen.

Work your long hours four days a week, but set aside one weekday and at least one weekend day to get away from your desk or home office to go out, have fun and meet people. You can go anywhere as long as there are men— or women— present. I know you have a lot of work to do. I assure you it will be right where you left it when you return.

"I realize my female friends who have no ambition or education or are willing to put up with men who treat them like garbage find men like leaves growing on trees. Are women who are educated, beautiful, and independent intimidating to men?"

To insecure men? Yes. There's also the type of man who finds the second batch of traits you listed as assets and would find a lack of ambition or education a turn-off.

The traits that men always list first as attractive in a woman are her nice-ness/nurturing and her support/loyalty. Education and ambition are great, but women overrate both when it comes to seeking a partner. It's what we tend to look for in men, but those aren't core traits that they look for in us. They're a bonus. The women you describe as lacking ambition and education are probably sweet and supportive, and that's what trumps for the opposite sex.

The women who put up with anything, have a lot of men *because* they put up with anything. They may have quantity, i.e., "like leaves growing on trees", but the men aren't of quality. Unless you want any ol' man no matter how he treats you just to say you have one, there's no need to envy your less accomplished friends.

"The 'men are intimidated by successful women' story is touted as a reason many women are single. I didn't believe it at all until it happened to me. I'm in my early 20s, not discouraged but shocked. What's your take on this?"

The core problem here isn't that a woman is successful; it's that a man is insecure. Don't bother trying to change him, accommodate him or play small to make him feel big. As soon as you identify this type of man properly, call it a wrap and don't look back.

It may not be the case here, but I do find that some successful women assume that any man who isn't interested must be the type of man I just described. "He's intimidated by my success!" has become a go-to scapegoat to make women feel better about themselves while they lick the wounds of rejection. It's also a way for women to avoid taking stock of how they played a role in the demise of a relationship.

Sometimes a guy stops calling or offers, "you're too busy" as an excuse because the successful woman he was seeking acted as if her salary or degrees were stand-ins for things that actually matter to him, such as attentiveness, spending time together and support.

The complaints I've heard from secure men about successful women are rarely about a woman's job, but about her inability to spend quality time; to turn off the critical, demanding "work mode" persona; and to know how to make a man feel that he's needed or appreciated. Some guys might bail because they're intimidated by your success, but some also lose interest because they don't like coming in second to a woman's job.

"I have tried dating guys who weren't at my level, career and salary-wise and their insecurities popped up. It became frustrating telling them that those things don't matter. I'm wondering if I should save myself the hassle! Is it wrong to seek guys who are, and have the same goals?"

It's not wrong to desire a partner whose accomplishments, income and goals are similar to your own (or bigger). Some might even say that on the surface, at least, that's an ideal partnership.

Still, I suggest that you not lump together all guys who are not at "your level" and assume that you'd have no chance at a healthy relationship with them. There is a type of guy who will make less than you and may be less educated than you, and he will be totally OK with that. He'll be happy to support you and be proud of your accomplishments and may be motivated by your success.

In addition, men who are as professionally accomplished as you are not automatically better and more secure. A guy "at your level" might feel threatened by your successes or salary or résumé, even if his are equal or better. He may began to treat you like a competitor, attempt to sabotage your success or begin to downplay your accomplishments.

I give you these alternatives to let you know that it's not the money, degrees or lack thereof that are the core problem with the guys you've dated recently— it's the insecurity. If career and salary and goals really "don't matter" to you as you say, then you can solve your dilemma pretty quickly by dating men who are more secure with what they do and what they earn. Unfortunately, it often takes a few months of dating to figure that out, but that's one of the points of dating anyway: to get to know people better and establish who is a good fit, *or not.*

"I am dating someone. We have strong mutual feelings, but he says he sees me "going places" and worries that he can't be by my side. Is it common for men to not enter relationships because of feelings of inadequacy? Can I convince him that he is perfect for me?"

Either he's giving you excuses not to commit, or he fundamentally just doesn't feel like he measures up. Neither bodes well for you.

Sticking around still wouldn't be your best move. The guy who thinks he doesn't have enough to offer, knows himself better than you do. Believe him when he tells you who he is. If he thinks he's not good enough, he isn't.

What happens when you stick around for this is you stunt your growth and stop being amazing you in order to make him feel better or equal. That doesn't serve you well. He will also begin to resent your success and do small things to sabotage or derail you to bring you down to whatever level he perceives himself on.

Take heed to what he said and get out now. You can find someone who sees you "going places" and feels like he deserves to be by your side because he's headed in the same direction.

"I'm dating a guy who's already established in his career and I'm still trying to establish myself in mine. I don't feel good enough to date him, I feel like I don't measure up. Can this work, is there something I need to do?"

We judge men's values by their security levels—height/size, career/money. Men don't value women for the same thing. Your career is the cherry on top. Whether you are nurturing/supportive/kind is the sundae.

Dating while insecure is a disaster waiting to happen. When you don't feel like you measure up, you tend to act out in self-destructive ways trying to gain approval (lack of value makes people do stupid things). Also, people who don't think they're good enough, tend to be whiny/needy/controlling. Like I said, disaster.

Work on getting your confidence up and building your career. Focus on what you have to offer instead of what you lack. It may help if you stop comparing your beginning to someone else's middle. Everyone has a starting point. You are at yours. There's nothing wrong with that.

"Guy I'm dating mentioned that he typically doesn't date women who don't make 100k or more. I don't make this. Should I dead him now or try to find out why he feels like this or what does it mean?"

Sometimes, and honestly, too often, people say things without really thinking about the impact or what it means. What he's trying to say in a round about way is there is a certain lifestyle that he wants to have and he wants a partner who can help him achieve that. Or he's one of those people who thinks that the "goodness" of a person is directly correlated with their salary, which is a faulty assumption.

Be honest with him about how your earnings fit into his preferences. And based on his response, make a decision about whether this is a relationship that has potential to move to the next level, if that's what you desire.

"I will graduate with a Ph.D. next year. Sometimes when I tell men, especially those with less education, they look the other way. How do I introduce my education/career to men without intimidation? I think it's their problem and not my issue."

If a guy bails because he perceives you as too smart for him, find, as Beyoncé would say, "the good in goodbye." You want the guy who hears you are getting a Ph.D. and is intrigued. The guy that suddenly loses interest? You weren't ever going to be able to hold a conversation with him anyway.

Introduce your accomplishments as something you are proud of. Mother Maya Angelou told us that we women do not ever play small to make someone else feel big.

"My boyfriend is thinking about marriage in 3 years and wants his first child before he turns 30. I'm 22 and thinking about my career. We love each other, but we seem to have different priorities? Help!"

Timing is everything in a relationship. You and your boyfriend should have a conversation to share your professional and family goals. You're not bound to operate on his timetable and you get a say in your life's trajectory, even when it's contemplating a life with him.

I wouldn't worry a lot about this right now, not at 22. As you get older, you learn that life rarely works how you map it out. You are both young and life, perspectives and goals change rapidly. Three years is an eternity, especially in your twenties.

Enjoy your boyfriend. When you two start having serious conversations about marriage, then it's time to hash this out in detail. In the meantime, offer a "*hmm, we'll see*" and go on and build your career.

If you were in the 30-ish range and having intense, spend-our-lives-together conversations, I would advise a much more serious conversation and compromising and negotiating on the timelines to get on a similar page *with each other*— it's not a dictatorship. You do get a say— and if you don't want *about* the same things, part ways.

"Met a guy in my grad program and dating for one year. Before I met him, I planned to live in Spain for a year, teaching English and traveling. He's upset and doesn't want me to go, but this has been my dream! I've traveled, but never lived abroad. And this is important to me. He brings up marriage and a future together. What should I do?"

If he wants to marry you, Spain won't change that. When a man wants you, he wants you. A year is a long time, but it isn't forever. If you're both dedicated to making it work, it can. Distance can be annoying, but it isn't that great a barrier for someone who wants to be with you.

When I was 22, I was living in New York, dating a guy from New York who was living in Washington, D.C. because he was still in college. He made plans to return to New York that summer and was looking forward to spending time with me. I got a job offer to work in London for the summer. It was a great (all expenses paid) opportunity and he didn't want me to go. He promised me the world and everything in it if I stayed.

I went anyway. The promise of marriage from a guy you're in love with is enticing, I know. But the kind of guy you want to marry, doesn't want you to give up your dreams just so he won't miss you.

Go to Spain. It's an amazing country. When I wrapped my job in London, I hopped on a plane by myself and did a 10-day, 3-city trek though Spain (Barcelona, Madrid, and Malaga). The trip changed my life. It may change yours too.

HIS CAREER

"I'm dating a guy who is very ambitious and always busy. He just asked me to be is GF, but he can't even be bothered to call me daily, just a text here and there. Should I drop him, or how do I get him to call more?"

Everyone's busy. The President of the United States is busy, but please believe he makes time daily for his wife and children because they are priorities to him. If this guy felt strongly about you, he would make time. He doesn't.

His focus is on his career right now, and he isn't able to juggle the responsibilities of his job with having a relationship, or a relationship just isn't that important to him.

You don't consider the guy who sucks at communication to be your man. He's not going to magically get better once you commit. In fact, he'll probably get more comfortable (read: worse) once he knows that you'll settle for mediocre treatment.

If you want to entertain this offer, tell him that you'll consider it once he begins to demonstrate traits that show he would make a good boyfriend. Otherwise, this a no-go.

"My husband has a bad habit of making plans with me and then work comes up and he cancels or is a bad mood, which ruins the night. I've told him I appreciate his job, but I need love too. He says I'm overreacting and not respecting he has to work. Any suggestions?"

Hubs is tripping, not because he's a bad guy, but because he's frustrated. We can work with him.

It sounds like you've already tried the sweet, "I support you, this is what I need from you" approach, but it fell on deaf ears. You're going to have to give him a come-to-Jesus talk. Let him know *that you miss him*, then add you didn't get married for him to check out on you for the job. When he comes to you with an issue, he expects it to be addressed, you expect the same courtesy, so you need him to take your complaints about the long hours or the bad mood seriously.

Now you're going to try something new. Instead of telling him what he's doing wrong and leaving him overwhelmed with how to fix it, tell him *exactly and specifically* what you want him to do to make you happy. Is it leave work on time (and doesn't bring work home) twice a week? Is it he takes you out on a weekend night and turns the work phone off? Whatever it is that you want, tell him *exactly and specifically* what that is.

"My husband and I are taking a late honeymoon. He is always on his phone for work and I told him to disconnect during the honeymoon. He got mad and irritated. Was I wrong?"

Yes. But not because you're frustrated by what he's doing. Admittedly, the person who's there, but really somewhere else because they live on their phone is terribly annoying. They might not mean to ignore you, but they are, and no one likes to be ignored.

Where you went wrong is "telling" your husband what to do. You would have gotten a lot further if you acknowledged how you appreciate the long hours he works to provide for/contribute to the household, then expressed how you feel when he brings his work home consistently. The truth is that even though he's physically there, you miss him and you should say that. Add that on your honeymoon, you want him to relax and then *ask* if he can take a break from the phone during the trip, or *at least* contain his calls/emails to a certain time period. (It's not like his job doesn't know he's away.)

One thing to add: if you're married to a high-powered, high-earning guy, the constant work is often the trade off for the power and money. This is a scenario where you have to choose your battles.

"I had a huge fight with my boyfriend and told him I wouldn't go to his annual work gala that night. After I said it, I regretted it and felt bad so I made steps to make things right. I got dressed for the event and finally went to his place. I get there, and his female friend, who always smiles and chats with me like she is my friend, is with him all dolled up. I tell him, 'I'm sorry, and I'm ready to go.' He says he would rather take her since she is reliable. She didn't even offer to stay. This is his big work gala. Why take just any woman? It means something. I am humiliated and mad at both of them. What should I do?"

Sorry. Not sorry. You got what you deserved. You acted like a brat by pulling out of an event at the last minute because you were mad, and you wanted to ruin your boyfriend's night. You knew what a big deal this event was and you canceled anyway. Your concern about how important the event is feels hollow after you discarded it like it was nothing .

Pulling out of an event on the day of is bad enough. It's worse that it was a work event. One of the core rules for operating in a healthy relationship is "do not embarrass your partner on the job," which you attempted to do. That's a big violation.

I'm not surprised he chose to go with her. When you changed your mind, you didn't call him to apologize and to discuss. You assumed that he would be at the house in a panic, and you expected to whisk in and save the day after you ruined it. You were caught off-guard when he made other plans that showed you were replaceable. You created a bad situation, and he made the best possible moves under the circumstances.

DATING AT WORK

Despite the prevalence of office hookups— 47 percent of people said they had observed a workplace romance, according to a study by employee-benefits provider Workplace Options— I'm no fan of them, and I'd actually discourage you from pursuing one.

That's not a popular opinion these days, since the same study found that 84 percent of employees ages 18 to 29 had no qualms about dating a co-worker. And many supporters of office hookups point to the fruitful marriage of President Barack Obama and First Lady Michelle Obama, which started in the workplace.

Still, I have to caution you. I haven't forgotten the drama at a previous job when a male co-worker was discovered to be dating three different women at the office, all while he had a girlfriend who was away at grad school. Talk about a mess! One of the women ended up throwing a cup of water *and the cup* on him in plain view of the entire office.

My general rule for dating in the workplace is, as an Ask.Fm reader once put it, "you don't get your meat where you get your bread", i.e, you don't get your dick where you get money. But if you want to do it anyway, let me help you avoid some common mistakes:

"I've seen you advise people not to date at work. Why? A guy at work asked me for my number. Does this dynamic matter? Or is it just a no-no all around?"

If this is the road you want to go down I have to ask you to consider some repercussions of deciding to proceed: if you have a negative experience while dating your co-worker, are you okay with seeing him everyday and working on projects with him? Will you be okay with your co-workers knowing that you are dating him? If he spreads your personal business to other co-workers, will that also be okay? Are you able to avoid being affectionate at work and using work devices (phones, e-mail) to communicate with him? Are you an expert at compartmentalizing?

If you can answer "yes" to *all* of these questions, proceed. And if you can't, thank your co-worker for expressing interest and decline.

"I have a serious crush on a co-worker. I'm not sure if he has a girlfriend. Any advice on how I can begin to drop hints so that it's not overwhelming, but I can get an idea if he's interested and available?"

My usual approach to dating is "no risk, no reward," and I encourage women to be proactive about making it known that they are friendly, interested and available to date. One of the ways to do so would be to chat up the guy you're checking for, and if the conversation goes well, casually suggest going to lunch together. If he's remotely interested, he will follow up. During the meal, you can ask him, "so, are you in a relationship?"

If he's tied up in a situation, keep things strictly professional going forward. (Being the other woman in general is bad enough. At the office, it's career suicide.) If he's single and interested, you'll know by the way he follows up. If he calls and/or asks to hang out again: he is. If he gives you the silent treatment or just the bare minimum of conversation: he's not. Can't read him? Err on the side of caution and drop it.

"I have a co-worker that I strongly care about. I do not want to date anyone else. He says that co-workers should never date and that I should teach at another school. We are both in our late 30s. What's the big deal? Why place rules like that? Should I leave my job?"

Ma'am! You're questioning changing jobs for a man that is not even your man, *not even your date.* You're not dating him, but you've decided you only want to date him. You don't have a commitment, but you want to be exclusive?

You are too caught up! Maybe he's the greatest ever. But he all but told you "no". LISTEN.

"I overstepped the line with my supervisor. We have slept in the same bed, kissed and cuddled. I've even seen him naked. Now, he won't return phone calls, and seems distant. What should I do?"

Start looking for a new job. You should never have sex with a co-worker who can affect your money and employment. But you have and now he's shading you because he doesn't want to be bothered anymore.

Unless you screw up on the job, it would be illegal to fire you. But he can. You can get a lawyer to fight the decision, of course, but you still won't have a job in the meantime. You've put yourself in a very vulnerable position. The sooner you can get out of that office, the better!

CHAPTER THREE

"What are we?"

I've heard rare stories of men who bring up the "where are we going?" conversation. In my experience, it's really early on, I barely know the guy and it's kind of creepy for him to ask since we've only known each other two weeks, if that. Every now and again, I'll hear from a woman who catches the guy she's dating refer to her as "my girlfriend" and a conversation about the relationship status, or lack thereof, stems from there.

In most of the scenarios I've heard, it's the woman who prompts the conversation of "what are we?" and a *discussion* about the relationship status stems from there. It's not the most romantic way of doing things, but it's practical— and less frustrating for you—to ask what you want to know and get an answer than be left in limbo.

Asking "what are we?" or some equivalent can be intimidating since we all fear rejection. The good news is that it won't kill you. And if you ask what you want to know, you spare yourself the nights sitting up wondering 'what if?' When you're fully informed about his interest (or lack thereof) you can make a decision that is *best for you.*

"I've been dating a guy for 2.5 months. What is a good amount of time to date before you label the relationship BF/GF?"

You don't just label it, you have a conversation with your partner about whether you're committed or not. And the ideal time is after you've dated about four to six months.

For the first three months you're dating someone you're dating their representative. The novelty of being around each other hasn't worn off and both of you are putting your best foot forward. After Month Three is when the butterflies start to die down and when the distractions of the world outside the relationship can no longer be kept at bay.

Before you commit to someone, you need to see them when they're stressed, overwhelmed, and/or dealing with family drama and work BS. Everyone's great when life is rosy. You need to see what they're like—and if you can deal—when hardships arise.

"You say that it takes time to know someone. Both sets of grandparents say it was love at first sight for them. I have held on to that notion since I was old enough to hear the stories. Do you say not possible because of modern times or do you completely not believe in love at first sight?"

I don't believe in love at first sight. You don't meet someone and suddenly know them well enough to build a life with them.

Your grands were lucky, or rare, or have brushed over some not-so-pretty details. I know several married couples that tell great "how we met" and "we always knew" stories, but I was there for some of those early stages. The current story they tell leaves out messy details like, "he was dating other women while he was my boyfriend, and I used to drive by his apartment to see if he was home". That doesn't have the same romantic ring as "it was love at first sight!"

Does it happen for some folks like your grands? Possibly. But finding "love at first sight" is not probable as a dating strategy.

"I've been dating a guy for about six months. He has cut off all other women and spends the majority of his time with me. I think we have a strong foundation, but he still refuses to be in a relationship with me. He says titles mean nothing to him. If the title is not there, are you actually in a relationship?"

But titles mean something *to you*. Your opinion counts here too.

You're in a grey area, not a relationship. You're also not "The One" to him. A guy who really wants you, wants to claim you. He feels pride in calling you "*my* girlfriend".

This scenario sounds like a guy who likes you and enjoys the perks of a relationship, but also still enjoys his wiggle room to do as he pleases, since technically, he's made no commitment to you. He'll go along with acting as a boyfriend as long as it's convenient for him. The second you ask of him something he's not keen on, he will remind you that he's not your man and leave you hanging. (Been there.) Either that, or you'll check his Instagram one day and see he has an actual girlfriend.

"I read something about a woman who was dating a guy for six months and he didn't introduce her when they ran into people. It got me thinking, does it matter if your boyfriend introduces you like 'This is Vivian' instead of saying, 'This is my girlfriend, Vivian'? Does saying 'girlfriend' first mean anything more than just saying the name?"

I'll probably upset a lot of "relationships" by saying this, but yes, the title means something "more." A title, or lack thereof, is one indicator about the seriousness of the relationship. It also changes the way you are treated and perceived.

Last summer, I attended a birthday celebration for a friend of my parents. Without fail, everyone we met introduced themselves and whoever they were with as, "my wife, Vivian," "my husband, Phillip" or "my daughter Ashley (or Hillary)." There's a reason for that. Not only does it establish the relationship, but it also gives a cue as to how you should respectfully proceed in engaging each of the parties.

"This is Vivian" tells the person that you're being introduced to nothing but your name. Vivian could be a co-worker or a random woman, and she could be fair game to approach about a date. "My wife" or "my girlfriend"— that is, claiming someone— lets the person you're speaking to know that there is a relationship in place and what kind. The title denotes the importance of the relationship. Titles are also subtle signals that say, "Hands off. She's taken. Do not approach."

"I've been dating this guy for five months. I asked him, 'Where are we going?' a little over a month ago and he kind of withdrew. We've still been going strong and I asked him again. He says he's not ready for a relationship, but he enjoys spending time and our daily talks. Should I hold out?"

I'm proud of you for asking for what you want, being patient while he mulled it over, and advocating again for what you desire. But he's given you his answer and it's that he's not moving forward with you. LISTEN!

"Holding out", or sitting around hoping for a different answer than the one you received, is also how you end up in the "grey zone", that hazy place where nothing is defined and the person who is the most emotionally invested gets crushed. You want "more", but staying put implies that you're okay with going through the motions of building a relationship, even if he's been honest about one not being on the horizon.

You're not okay with that, so let your desires and your actions be consistent. Thank him for his time, move on and lick your wounds.

"I started back talking to someone I parted ways with because he wasn't ready to commit, but my feelings about being in a relationship haven't changed. Do you think it's fair to say "all or nothing" in terms of a relationship? And what's the most effective way to express this without seeming like I'm giving an ultimatum?"

He's back. You still like him. But if he's still not willing to give you what you want, you're settling to keep him around.

Sticking around doesn't serve you if there's no relationship forthcoming. You like him and don't want to be "just" a friend. I mean, you could hang out with him and continue to have a great time, but all the while you'll be wondering, "but why won't he commit?" You'll be butt-hurt when he finds someone he does want to commit to.

The goal when you want a relationship isn't to settle for a piece of a man. It's actually to find someone who you get along with and who wants what you want. He enjoys your company, but he doesn't want to commit. Cut your losses and tell him to "holla" if he changes his mind. And you can lay it out to him plain just like that.

"I'm not exclusive with a guy friend because of distance. About a week ago, I met this guy and we just flow. I can finish his sentences. Now, he wants to be my only option. I don't know what to do."

Even if you were entirely single with no potential options, I would advise against committing to a man you met a week ago.

The chemistry is great and yes, that's rare to come by. But it takes more than chemistry to sustain a relationship. The hard truth is, you don't know him after a week. And if you're going to eliminate your other options, it needs to be for someone that you know is worth it.

Don't "X" him out though. Explain that you enjoy his company and you are having a great time getting to know him. Add that you may be interested in a relationship when you get to know him better, and if things continue to go well. Also, you would like to see him again soon. If he's really interested in a relationship like he says, he will put in the consistent effort to prove he's the real deal.

"I've been hearing "go with the flow" a lot. When a guy says this is he trying to keep you quiet for a while or does he mean let me take the lead on this and you just chill out'?"

It means, "I'm not ready." And perhaps he has a genuine reason. Many women jump the gun without knowing a guy well and want to rush into a relationship. Moving too fast doesn't benefit you or him.

If it's been more than 4 to 6 months, you're well within reason to ask "where is this going?" He may need to mull over his thoughts about being in a relationship, but he should get back to you in about a week with a definitive answer that lets you know whether he's ready or not. If you're hearing, "let me lead" after you've hung out for more than a season or two, it means he likes you, but he's enjoying his other options and isn't trying to commit *to you.* And that means it's time for you to move on.

"I wanted something more, he didn't. He insists on staying in touch. I've caught myself thinking this must mean something, but don't want to sell myself a dream. Am I setting myself up?"

You're setting yourself up *for failure.* He likes you well enough, but it does not mean he's going to commit if you *allow* him to stick around and try to show him how great you are.

There's something about you that he enjoys: your resources. I'm talking about your time, your energy, your attention, your emotional (but hopefully not financial) support. They are valuable even if they sometimes *seem* unappreciated.

Let me tell you how this plays out: he will still call all the time, wanting to unwind by you and wanting you to listen when he's had a hard day. And because you still hope this could turn into "something", you will let him come by and hear him out about whatever's on his mind. You will build him back up and you won't hear from him until the next time he's in need... of your resources.

He doesn't tell you, but he recognizes the value in your listening ear, your attention that makes him feel like a man, and the emotional support you deliver that makes him feel like it's all going to be okay. If you recognized the value of those traits, you wouldn't give them away to a man who won't commit to you.

"Found myself getting caught up so I want to take sex out of the equation. Plan to not put myself in compromising positions moving forward i.e., no sleepovers. Realistically, if I've already had sex with a guy (only a few times) but stop doing so in hopes of a relationship, is it too little too late?"

You're entitled to do what you want— or not— with your body at any time. But as a relationship strategy, this doesn't work. It's like you're playing a game and you're winning, then someone changes the rules to stop you from winning. It seems unfair and you don't want to play anymore.

You've already shown you don't require a relationship to have one of the big benefits, so asking him to exert effort to get something he received without any is asking a lot. At this point, he'll commit because he wants to, not because you're denying him sex.

"Currently trying my hand at dating and it's going well. However there are a couple guys I'd rather not hang out with again who are still expressing interest. How do you tastefully express disinterest?"

You have one of those First-World problems. God bless *you*, boo!

A simple call where you say, "I've been thinking, and I've decided this isn't going to work for me. I think it's best if we just part ways" works. After that, you're not obligated to answer the phone or respond to emails or texts anymore. That's blunt, but it's to the point and more importantly, *effective*.

THE BIGGER NEXT STEP

"We've been together two years and we're in our early 30s. Is it wasting my pretty to wait for a guy to finish school (another 18 months) to even discuss marriage? (His idea.)"

To just have a discussion about marriage?! Yes, it's entirely wasteful to wait that long to have a conversation about your future plans.

I understand— partially— where he's coming from. He's in school and probably uncertain about his postgraduate future. It's hard for a man to make a commitment to being a husband when he doesn't perceive his foundation as stable. The last thing you want to do is marry a man who isn't ready to be married.

But your guy isn't even offering any "When I... " or "If I..." plans to give you hope that a ring will be forthcoming. That's the bare minimum after you wait for 18 months. If he can't offer you that, there's no reason for you to be patient. If you have skills and luck on your side, you can meet another man—and a "good" one—and be engaged, if not married in the time frame your current man is offering just to *talk* about a ring.

"With my boyfriend almost seven years now. Things are going well, but it's bothering me that we're not engaged yet. We've talked about it a few times, but when I bring it up, he says he doesn't want to "ruin the surprise." That was six months ago. Should I put my foot down or just chill?"

Put your foot down. I don't like to put timetables on when a couple gets engaged. There are so many factors that play into readiness.

I am, however, comfortable saying 7 years is too long to still be wondering "if" and "when" about the relationship moving forward. People meet, get married, have two kids and divorce in less time.

You've got time and emotions invested in this man, but that's not enough if you want to be married and he's still dragging his feet after *seven years*. He's got to "make water or get off the pot", as my grandmother used to say.

You need to go to him and lay it out plain that after seven years you are ready to be married. Tell him how it makes you feel to be with someone for so long and he's still not ready to commit-*commit*. If he doesn't offer a timeframe for "putting a ring on it", or better, a wedding date (the ring is a romantic technicality) then you need to move on or accept being an eternal girlfriend.

"Been together a year. Asked BF where he sees this relationship going. He was stumped. Talked the next day, he said he's not a planner. I'm 35, have a 9-year-old, want marriage and more children. What would you do?"

I don't like "what would you do?" questions. It's not my life, it's yours. And we may not share the same values. You've said that want marriage and more children, and that's *your priority*, so you should work to have that.

The man you're with isn't going to propose to you anytime soon, if ever. "I'm not a planner" is a nice way of saying, "I'm nowhere near ready and have serious reservations about spending my life with you." A guy who is interested in marrying you, even if he isn't ready yet, would lay out the issues currently standing in his way and tell you how he's working to address them. He would want to give you some sense of security so you wouldn't bail on him.

Before you cut your losses, let's double-check to make sure he understands the impact of what he said. Communicate to your man how his answer made you feel. If he can express a plan, in the next 3 months, he needs to *show you* though his actions that he's working towards the goal. And if he doesn't have a plan at all? Go find someone who wants the same thing you do.

"Been living with my BF for 3 years now. We also have a baby together. I'm 29. He's 25. We talk about marriage plenty, but he always says, 'that's not my priority. I need to make moves and be financially stable first.' He says, 'maybe' in another 3 years marriage can be a possibility. Stay or go?"

You have a kid together, so my inclination (unless there's abuse or poor treatment) is always going to be to try to make it work, *if* he's putting forth the effort to work with you.

Being financially stable is something he should have thought about before he became a father. For whatever reason he didn't and the kid is here now. I'm curious, what, if anything he's doing to better his current situation? Is he in school, working on a promotion, holding down multiple jobs? Making moves on anything? If so, work with him, be patient, and continue to raise the child you share together.

If he isn't *currently* working toward something, then he's just giving you excuses and lip service for why he's not marrying you. Unfortunately, a lot of men didn't have healthy marriages or any marriages at all modeled for them. And others, are quite comfortable with the idea of having a "baby mama" as the ultimate level of commitment. If you want to upgrade from "mother of his child" to a "wife", you may need to change this relationship status from "girlfriend" to "co-parent" and find someone who is willing to make you a wife.

"My 2-year boyfriend is unsure about marriage. I love him but I am ready to marry and have kids. My ex has come back into the picture. He wants marriage, looks good on paper. I don't love him, but I am thinking to give him a chance because we want the same things now. How cruddy is it to dump boyfriend for ex just to marry and have kids?"

On a scale of 1-10? About a 12. But while you're thinking how "cruddy" it is to do to someone else, I'm thinking about what an awful thing it is to do to yourself.

You're anxious about getting married and the result is you're limiting yourself to two options, neither of which are ideal for you to meet your goals.

The ex only seems like a viable option because he gives you what your boyfriend won't. And while you're focusing on the marriage and the kids, you're overlooking the big picture. The ex is an ex for a reason. And whatever issues you had with him, him showing up and offering a marriage and some babies doesn't automatically resolve those past conflicts.

Also, understand the gigantic mess you are about to make being in love with one person, and hopping into a marriage with someone else. Oh, and at the point you're listing "he looks good on paper" as a reason to be with someone, you're not ready to be with *anyone.*

Marriage is more than just a wedding, a title, a social status and being a parent. If you want to have a healthy marriage or "just" an intact family to raise your kids in, you actually have to be able to build with your husband. Given whatever conflict you had with your ex that resulted in a break up, neither of you have demonstrated you can work through a tough issue with each other yet.

I respect your desire to be married and have children. But you've got some work to do on picking partners. When you're ready to move beyond the superficial, know that you can have someone who wants to marry you *and* give you some babies, *and* who you are in love with *and* who you can build a life with. Because you haven't met him *yet*, doesn't mean you won't ever.

"I love my dude and I know that he wants to marry me... soon! Is it normal to be a little afraid, particularly about my performance in the marriage? I've never had good examples of married women."

It's totally and completely normal. In fact, if you weren't worried, I would be for you. Marriage is a big commitment!

It will help tremendously if you communicate with your man about your fears and also find out what his expectations are for you as a wife. Give him the scenarios that bring up the most angst for you and talk them though. Theory is, of course, easier than application, but talking it though with the person you'll need to get through it with will alleviate some troubles down the line, as will set a foundation of good communication with your mate.

Also, you and your partner would be well served to find a *happily* married couple whom you can both relate to. You don't have an example, so ask who he knows, or look inside your church or any professional organizations you participate in to see who is available. Ask the couple to be your married mentors, of sorts. When you get to the hard times— and they will come— it's easier to get through them when you have an experienced listening ear to guide you back to the right path or steer you around mistakes before they occur.

"My other half and I have been together officially for 9 months. We got engaged 2 months ago. Everyone thinks we rushed it. I sometimes feel that way, but in the first month, I knew I was going to marry him. Do you think we are moving too fast?"

Congratulations! If you're in your early to mid-twenties, I'd say "yes". I wouldn't suggest you give the ring back, of course. Late twenties and beyond? I'd still say you were going too fast, but you've had a little more experience dating and you should have a better understanding of what works for you and what does not.

If you *know* after seven months that he's for sure "The One", so be it. At any age, given the quick courtship, I'd suggest you take a lengthy engagement to get to know each other better. The two consistent things that every married couple have said to me about marriage are: "it is hard" and "take your time. There is no rush." Listen to the people who have traveled the road you're getting read to walk down

CHAPTER FOUR

Me and You Against the World

My father likes to give random advice. Once, when we were randomly walking the streets of Miami on vacation, out of nowhere he says, "a man needs to feel needed, you know?" I'm accustomed to his randomness, so I didn't bother to ask where that came from. I humored him instead.

"What if I don't need a man?" I asked.

I figure I'm an adult with a job and my own place. I pay my own bills. At the time, I was single-single and doing just fine. I wanted a man, but *need?*

He explained, "whether you need him or not, he needs to feel needed or he will find someone who needs him."

I wasn't sold on his advice then. I am now. And largely because I observed that the women who act like they need their *partners* are the ones who are in healthy and lasting relationships.

That's up there with the best relationship advice I've ever received. And one of the many nuggets I've shared with readers and coaching clients over the years.

"I'm one of those women who gets things done and rarely stops to ask for help. Yet it seems women who are needy get all the attention. How do you show a man that he is needed?"

When you're in a healthy relationship, your man functions as your partner and to not utilize him makes him wonder why he is there. Sure, you can do everything alone, you've been doing it. But when you're in a relationship you don't *have to* do it all anymore. He's there to help and wants to, so let him.

What does that look like? When he's over, ask him to take the trash out, open the jar, get the thing off the high shelf (instead of climbing on the counter or straining to reach), clean the drain, fix the toilet, or carry something in the house. Just ask him to DO SOMETHING. Also, when something is going on at work, go over strategy with him to nail a presentation or ask for a promotion. Again, you don't need him to do these things, but isn't it nice to have two heads to brainstorm?

Don't worry about seeming needy. When a man likes you, he likes looking out for you. It gives him a sense of purpose. And he also likes bragging to other men about what you needed and how he came through for you. It makes him feel like he plays an important role in your life.

Last thing: be emotionally open (but only to men who have earned your trust). It's okay to let him know when you are scared, nervous, upset, etc. A man likes to feel you rely on him and you feel he can protect you. Do you need protection? Probably not. But you have someone there willing and able to help and protect if the situation ever calls for it. LET HIM.

"Do you think it's true that you have to give up your single ways when you're in a relationship? Other than seeing other people and flirting, of course. I don't want to become a new person in a relationship. Am I being unrealistic?"

If you're in a relationship, you can't act like you're unattached. People without partners can do whatever they want, whenever. You're not a prisoner in a relationship, of course, but you do have to have some accountability and make some compromises for the person you're with. You don't have to become a "new person", but you do need to treat your relationship like a priority.

That means that sometimes you will have plans with your man and your girls will call asking you to hang out at the most awesome event ever and you're expected to keep your commitment to your man. It means there are times you will have other plans and have to break them to go to his work event. It means you will sometimes want alone time, and will have to answer the phone to talk to him, even if it's just to tell him you're having a moment.

It also means you will have to be mindful of what you post on social media, not because you're being policed, but because you don't want to tick your partner off and you want him to show you the same courtesy.

Talk to your partner and ask what his expectations are and because it's a two-way street, share with him what you expect of him as well.

"I can't keep a boyfriend more than four months. What is wrong with me?"

I'd need to know if there was a consistent cause of the break ups to give you the best answer. But this scenario often happens for a few stand out reasons.

1. **When people rush into relationships without knowing the person they're committed to** and not allowing their partner to get to know them. Four months is around the time when people "stop being nice, and start being real." And that "real" person that you're showing is turning people off. I say, "you" only because you're the common denominator here.

2. You obviously don't have an issue meeting men and you're showcasing great traits that make them want to commit to you if you've been in multiple relationships. Is it possible that you're going the extra mile upfront to get his attention and **once you're comfortable in the relationship you're not showing the same interest?** If that's the case, you're going to have to step up instead of falling off. The old folks have a saying, "how you get him is how you 'keep' him." That means whatever you did to get his attention, you have to maintain that throughout the relationship.

3. **You're picking the same type of a guy,** namely one with traits that don't actually work for you. You'll have to analyze the type of guys you've been spending time with and figure out what they have in common. It might be something that you're attracted to, but if it's not getting you results, you're going to

have to let it go. In the future, when you see that trait(s), run!

"I've heard you say that girlfriends should not partake in wifely duties, but how do you become a wife without displaying wife-like qualities? How do you not act like a wife, if you're a girlfriend?"

First let's establish the Top 5 wife duties that are commonly mistaken for girlfriend duties. As a girlfriend (or for any other stage other than wife) you should avoid:

1. Providing financial support/ sharing bills/ co-signing loans, joint accounts/credit cards.

2. Giving keys to your home/car (unless there's an emergency).

3. Living together (explanation pg 171).

4. Having (more) children.

5. Befriending your partner's friends/ family (explanation pg. 249).

BONUS: sex without a condom.

My grandfather was a very traditional man and one of his favorite sayings was "Don't act like the wife, if you are not the wife." He passed that on to my mother, who passed it on to me. Loosely, he meant don't take on the responsibilities of a wife if you don't also get *the benefits.*

You can easily show your partner you have the qualifications to make a good wife without adopting wife responsibilities: You want him to see that you can keep a home? Keep your home clean, neat and organized when he visits. You want to show you're responsible, actually be responsible with *your own* affairs. That you're good with money? Be fiscally responsible with *your* money. Great with kids and nurturing? Play with his children/nieces/nephews/cousins and/ or pets. Oh, and be supportive of whatever's going on in his life, good days and bad.

At the same time that you're trying to prove you have what it takes to make a good spouse, make sure you are also observing your partner for his qualifications to be a good husband (just being interested and alive and a man is not enough). Is he hardworking? Does he blow his money on dumb ish? Does he refuse to go out to save money? What's his conversation and his character like? You go to his house often enough in a relationship, is it clean? Can *he* cook? Does he have a stable environment or does he move often? Does his cell phone get turned off? Do his cards get declined when you're out? The answers matter.

"Once we were in a relationship my boyfriend told me he's never been fully committed to anyone but me. It reminded me of that Beyoncé line, "foolish of me to believe that with

me you're a changed man." Is there such a thing as a reformed man?"

People can absolutely change, but it doesn't happen overnight or without some effort on their behalf. Ask him what's changed and what he's *doing* differently to avoid falling back into old patterns. If he doesn't have any solid answers, he's the same person he was before and you will see that not-so-pretty version of him soon enough.

"Do you believe that trust should be given at the beginning of the relationship until a reason is given not to? Or should trust be earned?"

By the time you're in a relationship, you should trust your partner, otherwise, why did you commit?

In any case, your trust is valuable and should not be given to just anyone who shows up in your life. It needs to be earned, and that should be done by evaluating the *consistency* of their actions *over time.* One-off occasions where your partner comes through, don't count.

COMMUNICATION

"You always ask, 'what do YOU want?', but what about compromise and seeing the other person's point of view. Is it really always all about you?"

I ask you to figure out what YOU want because it's the starting point of compromise and negotiation. If you haven't sorted through your feelings, how do you communicate to your partner how you feel? And if you don't know what you want, how do you communicate to your partner what you desire from them?

"I have trouble saying exactly what's on my mind for fear of seeming disrespectful or mean. How can I be more expressive without being afraid of hurting people's feelings or seeming rude?"

Plainly and evenly state what it is you want. If you don't advocate for yourself, you deserve and will receive nothing. Speaking up for yourself is not inherently "mean" or "disrespectful". The tone you use or your phrasing can be.

Some people will say they are offended or accuse you of being mean. It's because they aren't getting their way. Hold your ground. You are not obligated to accept whatever is offered or agree with everything said.

"He and I started off texting all the time. Two months later, I told him that he should call. He said we didn't start off calling, so he's never called. What is the logic behind this thought?"

Have you ever heard Oprah quote Maya Angelou's line, "you teach people how to treat you"? It applies here. What you wanted him to do in the beginning was pick up the phone, but you wanted him to like you, so you didn't rock the boat. In that time, you showed him that you don't require much effort from him to get your attention.

Months down the line, you're asking him to do more work than he's accustomed to doing for you. If he liked you more, he would have stepped up. You didn't ask him to walk on water, just to pick up the phone and punch a button.

Men are not dumb. They know they're supposed to call and they have no problem doing it for a woman they really want to talk to. Just like we enjoy the sound of some bass-y male voice in our ear, guys like to hear us to. It's more personal than a text.

Texting is what you do when you're busy doing something— or someone— else and don't want to be interrupted. He won't pick up the phone because he doesn't think you're worth the effort, and likely he's with someone else, possibly a live-in girlfriend or a wife.

You're fighting a losing battle here. Instead of trying to get him to change, stop dating him. And yes, it's fine to text him that you're moving on.

"Whenever I try to talk to my man, he gives me the deer in the headlights look. From sex to conflict resolution to daily wants and needs, nothing is connecting. And no, I am not bringing up these topics during the game or anything like that. He's just not getting it. Maybe not used to it?"

The onus of communicating in a relationship falls on *both* people in it. Unfortunately, the way communication usually plays out is a woman trying to communicate with her man and being frustrated that the attempts aren't working.

What you're saying is connecting, sort of. It's not like he doesn't understand the language you speak, it's either that he doesn't care of doesn't know what to do about it. You can't work with a man who doesn't care. So let's just hope that your man doesn't know what to do, but would put forth some effort if he did.

Instead of telling him what's wrong, which he just hears as complaining, come to him with solutions. You don't like when he does X, tell him, "you know what I would really like? Y." That way he knows what to do. Also, after you make a suggestion about what you want, ask him, "so, what do you think about that?" to get feedback and involve him in the solution you've offered.

"Guy I'm seeing wants me to express interest in him more. He told me, "I had a great time with you" and I responded, "I'm glad you did." He says that doesn't let him know if I had a great time. I like him a lot, but I am a fan of taking it slow and not getting all caught up. Am I wrong or is he over-thinking it?"

You're wrong. Your answer was cold. Since you like him "a lot", the right answer was something along the lines of, "I had a great time too. Looking forward to seeing you again."

I'm all for taking it slow, but you're not doing that. You're showing him, albeit unintentionally, that you're not interested and don't appreciate him. He's not going to stick around long if you keep this up.

There's nothing wrong with him knowing that you like him. That's not rushing. Sex too soon is rushing, turning over all your free time and forgetting about the life you had before you met him is getting caught up. Committing to a person you barely know is going too fast. Telling a guy you had a good time on a date is giving him the encouragement to ask you out again.

You've put up a wall and I get why— you don't want to be hurt. But when you're callous for no apparent reason, you won't get the love, attention and affection you want either.

"My boyfriend sometimes doesn't answer his phone or call me back when I call. I've told him it irks me, and he'll get better but then goes back to doing it. We've been together 6 months. The rest of the relationship is fine, but we can go up to a week without talking."

It's impossible for the rest of the relationship to be okay when one of the core traits you need for a healthy relationship— communication— is *severely* lacking.

Not only does it sound like you're boyfriend isn't interested— interested men call even when they don't want anything because they want to hear your voice or tell you something funny/crazy that happened or just to "check-in"— it also sounds like he may be seeing someone else.

We're all attached to our phones, *all the time.* Your boyfriend sees his ringing, but chooses not to answer, or even respond up to a week at a time, either because he doesn't want to offend the other person he's with who may not even know about you or he just doesn't want to be bothered by you. Sorry.

"We all know that you can't make anyone do anything and this is very frustrating. It's understandable to break up with a BF if they don't eventually comply but how does one deal with the frustration and lack of action when it's a spouse?"

I wish we all knew that. Do you know how much easier my job as a dating coach would be, if I had a job at all anymore?

With a husband, you choose your battles the same way you do if you're a girlfriend who wants to upgrade to fiancée/wife. Your spouse is going to do things that you don't like and that you strongly dislike. The stuff that drives you absolutely nuts and goes past your line of what's acceptable, bring it up with your mate and ask, "how can we solve this together?"

Hopefully, you picked a guy who communicates well, wants to see his wife happy, and is willing to do his part to make the relationship work. He gets that if you're unhappy, the relationship isn't happy and he's got to step up and work *with you* to get things back on course.

Of course, there will be times when what you want is in direct opposition to what he wants. You'll have to compromise or one of you will have to bite the bullet and put maintaining the relationship before your wants. That's what marriage is sometimes. Ideally, you both take turns giving in. And if it's always one person compromising, your issues are bigger than whatever you're currently disagreeing about.

And finally, if you can't work it out as a couple, go to a therapist to see if a professional can help find a middle ground to save the marriage. Hopefully, this step will help you to find clarity about your priorities and communicate with your spouse better to solve the problem. If therapy (and a lot of hard work from both of you) doesn't fix the issue, your options are to stay in the marriage, hope things get better and deal the best you can, or leave.

"I read a book that said men respond to no contact. When my guy is messing up— despite attempts to tell him— I let him stew with no word. Then, I'm hit with the 'are you seeing someone else?' line. What gives?"

Admittedly, what I am about to write is going to sound both ironic and horrible coming from an writer/blogger/author, but: don't believe everything you read.

You don't improve communication (or get results) in your relationship by giving your partner the silent treatment. That book gave you bad advice, evidenced in your man's response. He's messing up, and when he's finally ready to talk, it's not about the issue you have, but something he feels you did wrong. Your issue gets lost in the antics and gets addressed on the back end, if at all.

None of the ways you are trying to communicate with your man are working, so it's time to try something else. Spare yourself the guessing games and just ask him, "when I have something that I need to talk with you about, what's the best way to bring it up to you?" Let him tell you what works for him, and if it's reasonable, give it a try. Whatever he suggests will go over better than what you've already tried.

"Sometimes I act like I don't care, but I really do. Like, if a guy cancels plans and I really want to see him, I won't say it because I don't want to sound needy. How do you balance coming off as needy versus telling a guy how you feel or asking for what you want?"

If you're not willing to ask for what you want, you can't reasonably expect to get it, nor do you really deserve to. *Ouch!* I know.

If you want something from your partner, you have to tell him. And if you're disappointed you have to speak up. If you act like him cancelling on you— it happens, but should not be a habit— isn't a big deal, then he will continue to do it and not think twice about it, because you've treated it like it does not matter to you.

In pretending you don't care, the message you're sending is that you have no standards. The proper response to him cancelling plans (the first time) was, "I was looking forward to seeing you. I'm a little disappointed. When are you going to make it up to me?" That would tell him, nicely, that you're interested in him, you're not happy about the situation, and you expect him to keep his word.

"Needy" is the least of your worries. That term is only used to refer to women who are emotional wrecks and throw tantrums when they don't get their way. And so often, they seem to have a partner. Work on asking for what you want. A guy who is interested will either figure out how to get it done or just simply tell you upfront that he's not able, so as not to disappoint you on the back end.

"Doesn't telling a guy what we want cheapen whatever it is we're asking for? After years together, shouldn't he know the woman he is with?"

I mentioned this in the previous chapter, but it's worth reiterating: men are not mind readers. They're also, as one guy I interviewed put it, "not women with penises."

Your man doesn't think like you. He's not *you*, and he's not a woman. Men have a whole different— not worse, not better— train of thought going on in their heads. Things that are blatantly obvious to you, and maybe to other women too, just bypass them sometimes.

Relationships are a process and you're always learning something new about your partner as they grow and evolve. If there's something that you want from him, spare yourself the frustration of hoping he'll figure it out, and just ask him for whatever it is. That will tip the odds in your favor of getting it.

"You often say ask someone what they want to do. But can't someone not have a solution and just be upset and that not be a bad thing? Does every relationship issue have to have a sit down conversation to talk about wants and needs? Can't someone just be upset and not necessarily have a solution or alternative?"

Being upset from time to time is completely normal. However, when you don't address the things that really tick you off, and you try to overlook them, and just pretend they didn't happen, you end up blowing up over something that's not even what you're mad over.

If you've ever heard that cliché story about the couple who has a big blow up over squeezing the toothpaste from the bottom versus the top, what they're angry about isn't really toothpaste. The real issue is all the things they were also mad about and have built up resentment toward their partner over.

Healthy and happy couples communicate *a lot*. It's much easier for them to get along when they address their issues, problem-solve and find solutions day-to-day when someone is just upset or slightly annoyed about one thing than when the person is in a rage about everything

CHAPTER FIVE

Looking for Trouble

If you've ever read anything I've written on snooping (or you watched Bravo TV's *Blood, Sweat & Heels*), then you know my position: this is ludicrous. Snooping is often done under the guise of getting necessary information. What it really is, is a lack of trust, so-called "trust issues" (insecurity) and a desire for control.

There are various ways that people snoop, from hacking into phones and email, combing through social networking accounts to adding spyware to computers, or tracking devices to electronics, rummaging though drawers or pockets, and even driving by houses to check if the lights are on or off, whose car is in the driveway or if anyone else's is parked nearby (full disclosure, I've ridden shotgun with a friend more than once at 3AM to check on her man).

Obviously, I'm no fan of snooping, but lots of people have done it. Thirty percent of dating couples and 37 percent of spouses— slightly more women than men— say they have checked their partner's email or call history, according to a survey by the electronics site Retrevo. Among those under 25, almost half reported snooping.

What all of those amateur private investigators didn't realize is that they could have saved themselves the trouble. In the same Retrevo study, just 9 percent of snoopers found confirmation of infidelity. But there's an even bigger reason not to snoop: by the time it gets to the point where you can't trust your partner and you have to go on the hunt to verify what they say, your relationship is doomed. Even if you snoop and your partner isn't up to anything, when you get caught, you're now the one violating the trust in the relationship.

You would have been better off talking with your partner about your concerns. If you can't get reassurance or resolution through communication, then it is better to walk away. And if you're one of those people who is in doubt about every partner, skip the energy spent on digging thru their stuff and look up the contact information for a good therapist instead.

Peep what these "very curious" women are up to:

"I have trust issues. I look for things. Dating a guy since March. After some time, I started to ask if he was seeing someone else. I came upon his password for Facebook and email. I found out he's a swinger and has been seeing and sleeping with other women. I feel guilty for invading his privacy, but I want to confront him."

I respect so much that you're upfront about your baggage. But it's not enough just to acknowledge it. You have to work on it too. And when you have trust issues that haven't been resolved, you don't need to date.

You may have been right about the guy you were seeing, but you're still wrong here. You weren't in a committed relationship; he's free and clear to date other people, though he should have been honest with you when you asked. But not trusting him does not give you the right to violate his privacy. It does give you the right— which you always have— to say, "I don't think you're being honest with me" and to stop dating him.

I'm unclear on why you want to confront him. You found out that he's up to some business you want no parts of. Do you just want him to know that you know? (That's your ego.) Do you want him to apologize? (Not likely, especially when he finds out you hacked him.)

Spare yourself the messy battle. Tell him that you're not interested in seeing him anymore, get tested for sexually transmitted infections since he's been with all these other women, and get a therapist to help you work on your trust issues, so at the very least, you learn that if you can't trust your partner, *you can still trust your instincts.*

"My boyfriend has condoms in his drawer. We don't use them. One came up missing. I didn't say anything about it. I just realized that he put the missing one back. (No, I didn't miscount.) Although I'm glad to see it back, how would you feel about that? Was he gonna cheat but changed his mind?"

You're thinking he was going to cheat and didn't. I'm thinking that he did and just replaced the condom that he used. Or worse, he cheated, and didn't use one.

I don't understand why you're with this man, or why you were having sex with him, even before the condom went missing. You clearly don't trust him not to cheat, which is why you've been counting condoms. But despite not trusting him to be faithful, you don't require him to wear condoms when he has sex with you. Why not?

Whatever happened with this traveling condom, you need to talk to your boyfriend about fidelity or his lack of it. It's a long overdue conversation that should have happened when you discovered a condom was gone, or better, when you felt like you had to snoop because you don't trust him.

Infidelity and sexual health are nothing to bury your head in the sand about. And not only do you have to bring up the condoms, you can't have sex with him until both of you are tested for sexually transmitted infections, including HIV, which can take up to three months to show up in a test.

"My ex used to go through my phone when I would leave the room, and it would piss me off. He never found anything because I was being faithful to him. I decided to put a lock on my phone because I felt disrespected, now he's pissed. What do I do now?"

Putting a lock on your phone is a passive-aggressive way of saying, "This is not OK." To someone who already has trust issues, the pattern change of you locking your phone just made things worse in what was already a no-win situation for you.

Snoopers have severe trust issues that they likely picked up after being cheated on. Going through emails, cell phones, voicemails and stalking their significant other (and all potentials for the position) on social media is their twisted way of protecting themselves from being blindsided again. Their position: If you don't check to see if your partner is not cheating, then how do you really know they are faithful?

You need to have a frank conversation with your boyfriend about his snooping. It's imperative that he knows that you're not comfortable with him going through your phone, not because you have something to hide but because you find it disrespectful. It also reveals that he doesn't trust you, and that is a huge problem in any relationship.

Your mate is clearly insecure, and it may be about something he's observed in the relationship that he doesn't know how to address in an effective way. Talk to him and see if you can pinpoint the reason behind his behavior *with you.*

The "with you" is important. If something has occurred in the relationship that's left him insecure, it can likely be addressed with better communication and transparency. However, if he just has a general distrust of women, and this is what he's always done, his actions are more about his baggage with trust and control, which he will need a therapist to dismantle.

It's unfortunate that he has these issues, but it's a big (and irrational) problem, and you are not obligated to put up with it.

"I went through my boyfriend's phone and found out he's been talking to his ex-girlfriend, who he told me he hadn't been in contact with. He's calling her pet names like "babe" and "sweetheart"— the same things he calls me, reminiscing about their past sex life, and the phone log shows they've been talking a lot and they've met up at least once. Last Friday, I was calling him and he didn't answer his phone. He told me he'd left it at home, but his texts indicate he made plans to go to dinner with her. I want to confront him, but I don't want him to know how I found out. Help!"

You thought your boyfriend was up to something, and unsurprisingly, he is. You've found proof that he's been lying to you about being in contact with his ex and his whereabouts, and that he's been cheating on you. (What you call "made plans" is actually a date with his ex; call it what it is.) The cute names he calls her and "remember when" conversations about their sex life indicate he intends to make her a bed buddy again, if she's not already.

I'm curious as to what you hope to gain from a confrontation. You thought strongly enough that he was cheating to check his phone, and now you know you were right. Would an apology make everything better now? Do you want to work on a relationship with someone you don't trust? Those are questions only you can answer.

If an apology is what you're expecting, you're asking a lot of a man who ignored your call while he was likely on a date with another woman, then lied to you about it. When confronted, he's more likely to follow the first rule of the cheating handbook, which is, "When Caught, Deny, Deny, Deny." You're likely to get a rambling and confusing explanation of how everything isn't what it seems. Or better, he switches the topic to you violating his trust.

You may be hopeful that the relationship can be salvaged— what your desire for a confrontation is probably about— but it's clear that your cheating boyfriend wants to date other people because he has already started dating, and possibly having sex with, his ex. What's best is to skip the confrontation and just break up with him with no explanation. You can avoid additional drama, and if you're seeking some sort of payback, it's also the best way to screw with a person's head.

"DAYUM! I'm so tired of women getting blamed for looking through phones. Yes, it's sneaky. Yes, she knew something was wrong, but why should she have to forgive him of at least emotionally cheating when he flips the script on her?"

Violating someone's trust is wrong and you can rightfully be called on it. Snooping on someone is a HUGE violation of trust. And when you snoop and find information, you are putting yourself in a conundrum. He did wrong and now you also did wrong. Two wrongs don't make YOU right.

She doesn't have to forgive him. There's no obligation. But when/if he forgives her for a huge violation, in the moment, it's really hard to say, "well thank you for overlooking my massive screw up. That was very big of you, I, however, will not do the same."

You're talking about a kind of woman who didn't trust herself to think something is up, have a conversation, then go with whatever her gut said after. You get some surprises, of course, but in general, the type who snoops isn't the type who will stand on her own two feet after she finds what she looked for and say, "I'm done!" If that were the case, she would have skipped the confrontation after she thought something was up and after she found evidence. She's still trying to un-believe what she saw.

"I have been dating a guy for a few months and decided to Google him and search public records because I suspected he was lying. I confronted him with this information and now he feels betrayed even though he lied. He says

he was going to eventually come clean. Can we get past this?"

What you did doesn't count as snooping or betrayal. You didn't dig through his clothes, or hack into his phone or accounts, you used readily available resources on the Internet to learn the truth. That's fair game.

You're asking "can we get past this?" The answer is "maybe". But I'm asking, "do you really want to?" Your guy lied to you, straight up. And despite what he says, it's far-fetched that he was going to "eventually" tell you after lying for months.

I'm going to guess that if you went through the trouble of debunking his story, he didn't lie about an inconsequential detail. It was likely along the lines of his current marital status or his arrest record.

Whatever he lied about, use this barometer to decide whether you can move forward: "do I currently trust him?" "Is continuing to date him in my best interest?" If you can't answer "yes" to *both* questions, then you shouldn't stick around.

CHAPTER SIX

I Hate You So Much Right Now!

Couples argue. If you never disagree, you're suppressing a lot of issues, and they're going to come out any day now. Despite what's shown in Hollywood romances, dating and relationships aren't always pretty. They can get very, very ugly. And it's entirely normal to have blow ups that aren't neatly wrapped up in 60 to 90 minutes.

The good news is that short of any kind of abuse, if you and your partner are both willing to put in the effort to resolve an issue, then most— not all— problems can be worked out. And the bad news is some issues just aren't worth resolving.

When you argue with your partner, do yourself a favor and focus on the actual problem that needs a resolution. Try to avoid all the name-calling, bringing up old, un-related drama that was supposed to have been resolved (but isn't), talking negatively about your partner's family (especially children), and/or making unsubstantiated accusations. And if you can also manage not to yell —hard, I know, but completely ineffective and escalates the situation— you will have much shorter arguments that will get resolved faster.

All of this is easier said than done, but *not impossible* with patience and practice.

"Is it realistic for couples to always fight fair? I've heard you say walk away and cool down, but sometimes I just have to address it right there when I'm pissed."

It's entirely realistic and it can happen, maybe not always, but *most of the time, with practice*. Many of us were not raised in households where our parents— if they were both there— practiced good communication. We heard yelling and swearing, and big blow-ups. For some, that was the rule, not the exception.

You don't "have" to address it when you're pissed. You want to because you're in your feelings. Based on the number of times you've gone off while you were angry, how many of those times got you the result that you really wanted? You wanted someone to treat you better or recognize that they wronged you in some way. But when you were screaming and cursing, didn't it just make them defensive and indignant about giving you an apology?

There are other ways to communicate with your partner, ways that don't leave you angry, exhausted and drained and still with unresolved issues when an argument is "done."

"I've read Ask.Fm for months now. Lots of your advice says "be nice" or "say things nicely". Makes sense, but when I'm upset/angry/hurt that sometimes overrides what I know is the most effective method. How do you remain nice even under stress?"

Admittedly, it's hard. When I'm upset/angry/hurt, I'm just in my feelings. And I have a tongue that I can wield like a weapon. Knowing this, I make a conscious effort not to have difficult conversations when I don't have a level-head. And if they're forced upon me (because you know some people just have to speak on *their* time and *their* terms), I listen and ask (out of courtesy, not permission) if we can discuss it later when I've had time to calm down. This small difference significantly changed the personal relationships in which I had conflict.

Another tip: prepare for conflict. Disagreements are one thing you can guarantee will happen, so create an action plan when you're unbothered for how you will respond. Try this: "the next time I am angry, I will _____" Anything that doesn't involve you blowing up and making a stressful situation worse works. Also, don't beat yourself up, if you don't get the hang of it right away. Change is a process.

"My friend told her boyfriend to go away during an argument and he did. He hasn't called in two weeks. Presumably, they are broken up. I say this just gave him the out that he was looking for. As mean as it was to say, he would have surfaced after awhile if he really wanted to be with her, right?"

Wrong. There are certain things you don't say or do to people even when you are mad. And treating a person as if they're trash that can easily be set out is on that list.

Maybe he wanted out, maybe not. I can't tell based on the question. I do know that unless the guy has royally and gigantically screwed up and feels like he deserves to be treated that way, no self-respecting man is going to stick around after a woman says that or come back to her once he leaves. Really wanting to be with someone doesn't mean putting up with being treated any ol' way just to stay there.

I know folks get pissed, and anger inspires all sorts of bad decisions, but anger isn't a justification for being an a—hole. She treated her relationship like it was nothing to her and told him to leave. He listened to what she said. I'm unsure what else she expected to happen.

"During a fight about money, my husband called me a "leech" and "dead weight". I still can't believe it and we haven't said a word to each other since. I don't know how to begin to fix this. What do I do?

What happens when you get to screaming and name-calling, as you know, is that it derails whatever the *conversation* is supposed to be about. And when the actual issue finally does get resolved, there's no "win' if your partner is still pissed (i.e., hurt) about what you said days, weeks, months, or even years prior.

Tell him you're still upset, that it's not OK to call you names when he is angry and you want an apology. You need to follow up that chat with a discussion about appropriate boundaries when you two argue.

You also need to have a conversation with a level-head about how much he actually meant what he said. It's clear that he doesn't think you're pulling your weight in the relationship, so what does he want you to do to step up here? Ask him to start the conversation.

"My boyfriend and I fought pretty bad for a few days and some of the argument was in text. We have made up and I now wish both of us would erase the mean messages. My boo says to keep them as a reminder. What would I need a reminder of mean stuff for?"

You don't need a reminder, and neither does he. He's keeping it either because while he might be over what ever the argument was about, he's not over what ever additional— and mean— words were said while you were arguing. It's a reminder of how ugly you, and he, can get when you are both angry.

Just as an aside, try not to argue on text or via email. The impersonality of the mediums practically encourages people to say things more harshly than they would to someone's face.

"My fiancé says that when we argue I sound like my mom, who he says has no respect for men. I don't agree and feel he's using this to shut me up in arguments. Is this worth examination and changing my argument style? Or do you think he's just using that as a war tactic?"

Your disagreements with your partner, someone you love and who is supposed to love you, shouldn't be described as "war". Arguing isn't about winning. You're supposed to be solving an issue, not one-upping each other.

Given that you think of an argument with someone you love as "war", you probably do sound like your mother. When emotional, people tend to default to familiar behavior— good or bad. Your fiancé's assessment is worth examining. Guys don't stay where they don't feel respected by their woman.

"My boyfriend and I had and explosive argument the other night. I believe alcohol caused a lot of hurtful things to be said. We kissed and made up, but I'm still bothered by some of the stuff that was said. Should I bring it up or blame it on the alcohol?"

Whenever possible, avoid arguing when you or your partner have been drinking, even a little bit. (If you're the type that likes to argue when you're drunk, you don't need to drink.) Alcohol tends to give everyone loose lips and dulls the ability to determine when you're crossing the line. That "explosive" argument likely would have been milder if you were both sober.

That said, alcohol can also act as a truth serum of sorts. Sans filter, people let out a lot that's on their mind that they might otherwise hold in, or at least would have said in a less offensive way. Blaming it on the alcohol doesn't erase the issues. They are still there even if they aren't acknowledged. And they still bother you.

Remind your guy that you're not mad any more, but you are concerned about some of the things that were said the other night and you would like to work on addressing each of your concerns while sober.

"BF and I had a fight and haven't spoken in two days. I always call to make up. I know communication goes both ways, but I feel like if I didn't do anything wrong, I shouldn't have to be the one to extend the olive branch. I want him to show some effort. I know it's his pride. Is that the wrong way to look at things?"

Yes. You want to be right *and* happy, and sometimes you don't get to be both. If you have to choose, go with "happy" and pick up the phone. Making the first move has been your role in the relationship for its duration. If you want to change this make up ritual, you can, but you can't do it until after this current argument is resolved and the new course of action is discussed.

Call him. There's no need to apologize if you've done nothing wrong, so just open up the lines of communication so you two can get back on solid ground.

Give a couple days for warm and fuzzy feelings to return, then tell him what's on your mind about him not putting forth effort when there's discord, and how you need him to step up.

"When my boyfriend and I argue, he won't talk to me for a couple days, and talking is always on his time. How much space should a woman allow a man during an argument or a stressful time?"

Choose your battles and let him be. He'll call you when he has something to say. Go on with taking care of whatever business you have and let him pick up the phone when he's ready. Pushing him to talk on your terms because you are ready is about wanting control, not problem-solving. Focus on what will help you get the problem solved.

He needs space to either sort out his thoughts because he's not good at spur of the moment conversations, or he gets pissed and will come out of pocket when he's mad. Waiting to hear what he has to say can be annoying, but 48 hours is still reasonable (if you said 4-7 days, I'd call "foul".) You would rather deal with him when he has something constructive to contribute and is ready to address the problem, than be on the other end of him being reckless.

"I love my boyfriend, but he never wants to compromise when we have an argument. He thinks he is always right, even when he's not. He still believes that the man has the authority in every relationship. How can I get him to realize that this is a new day?"

You can't. He doesn't respect women very much based on your description. It's going to take another man to get through to him.

You should not stick around waiting for him to realize the Stone Age is over. I know you love him, but you have to love you too. And that means not being in a relationship with someone who has made it clear he doesn't respect you or your opinion.

"I was crying out of frustration that my BF wasn't understanding my perspective and that we were having so many issues. He asked, 'Are you really crying?' then hung up on me. It's been a day and he hasn't called or texted me once. This is hours after him saying how much he loves and cares for me. What gives?"

Many men are uncomfortable with woman-tears. They don't know what to do when a woman starts crying. When you started crying, he thought you were making too big a deal out of an issue he didn't understand, and thought you were using tears to get him to give you your way.

A male reader wrote in once with the other perspective of a similar incident: "New woman I'm seeing cries during arguments, runs in bathroom and hides to avoid arguments. I, and many of my boys, hate these antics. Why do so many women think crying or playing these games will work? It's so unattractive."

This is probably along the lines of what your boyfriend was thinking when he hung up. Call him and have a conversation about the tears. Explain that when you cry it's because you're upset, not because you're being manipulative. It's going to happen from time to time, and it's not okay for him to hang up on you or be dismissive of you when you cry. If you can't get an apology, get a new boyfriend.

"When my fiancé and I argue, he talks over me loudly, mocks me by repeating what I say, or says "blah, blah, blah" while I'm talking, rolls his eyes and walks away. This frustrates me to tears. I've asked him to stop but he won't. Otherwise he's a great guy. Any suggestions?"

He's not otherwise a great guy. He might look good on paper, but you don't go from being a so-called great guy to this level of appalling behavior in a smooth and easy transition. The way he dismisses you and belittles you definitely shows up in other places in this relationship.

He doesn't like you very much, despite putting a ring on it, neither does he respect you and nor does he care about your feelings. A man who remotely cares about you doesn't bully and dismiss you when you try to talk to him.

You can't marry him as long as he behaves this way. It will only get worse, and possibly physical. Tell him he either stops *and you both go to therapy* or you give him his ring back

.

CHAPTER SEVEN

The Ghosts of Exes Past

Nothing quite strikes fear in the heart of some women as another woman knowing her man better or longer than her. In most cases you have nothing to worry about. If he really wanted to be with his ex, he probably would be. But even the most confident among us get curious about her sometimes: *What was she like? What did she look like? What did she do that I don't? Do you ever think about her?*

It would be easier perhaps, if you were your ex's first girlfriend, if there was no one for him to compare you to or no one that had his heart before you. But for most of us, that's not the case. And in insecure moments, "She" might seem like a threat, even if she isn't—and has no interest in being—one.

So how to deal?

"Is it important to know how a man treated his former girlfriends? My bestie says, "yes!" I say, "no" because a man will treat a woman how she allows him to treat her. Your thoughts?"

You're both right. If he has a track record of being a horrible person and there's been no great event to give him a wake up call or he hasn't had a stretch of time to pull himself together, he will more than likely treat you the same way he did every woman before you.

But your point is valid as well. He will treat you horribly whether you have standards or not because that's just what he does. But if you have standards, you won't stick around and the bad treatment will be a one-time deal rather than an ongoing occurrence.

"When my fiancé and I are out, I often catch him looking at women who look more like his ex than me. It makes me feel some kind of way. I try to ignore or look away because I

know all men look, but it still makes me feel insecure."

Unfortunately, your man's reckless eye-balling is an issue that a lot of women chalk up to "men being men." It's deeper than that, though. It's profoundly disrespectful to ogle other women, and it's additionally disrespectful to do so when your partner is present.

You're right. Men look. And women do, too. "Committed" doesn't mean "blind". But when he's looking hard or long enough that you, his partner, take notice, it's a big problem. And though a small act, it could have big implications for how he feels about you.

Tell him how it makes you feel when he does it. If he remotely cares about you, he'll quickly adjust his ways.

It's not at all your fault that he does this, but your silence condones his behavior. If he doesn't change immediately, call him out when you catch him staring at other women, instead of looking away in embarrassment or ignoring it. "You know I'm standing here, right?" "Do you know her? Because you're staring", or "Excuse me, you're being rude" are all acceptable reactions.

"My boyfriend is friends with a couple of his exes who are still in love with him. I feel his bonds with them make it hard for him to put the required energy into building *us*. Should I have to compete with women from his past?"

No, you should never feel like you have to compete with other women who are in your man's life. It's entirely unacceptable for him to be in a relationship and befriend women whom he knows still have feelings for him. It makes you insecure and it gives the women hope that the current friendship can turn into a relationship again. It's just sloppy.

If you don't feel like he is all-in with you because of his relationships with these other women, then you need to tell him to let go of his exes to focus on his present girlfriend, or you're out (if you say it, you have to mean it or it undermines your credibility). If he's unwilling, change boyfriends. You can't build a healthy relationship on a foundation this shaky.

"My boyfriend is close to his ex. In general, I don't care if my guy is friends with an ex, but he is cagey with me about the nature of their relationship and gets upset when I ask questions. Is he hiding something?"

Probably. Part of the deal with having opposite sex friends or being friends with exes when you're in a relationship, is being transparent with your partner about conversations, communication and the friendship in general, to put them at ease. He's not doing that.

Something is going on with their relationship that he doesn't want you to know about.

Talk to him about it and see what he says. If you can't get a straight answer, it's time to offer him a choice: you or the ex. And if he can't make a choice, it's time for you to go. When another person is coming between you and your mate, and your partner can't let that other person go, it's best to leave the two of them to their own devices.

"I just found out my husband reached out to an ex-girlfriend who caused problems while we were dating. He says he was curious to see how she was doing/where she is in life. Of course, I'm pissed because she easily gets the wrong idea and won't go away now that he's reopened the door. What do I do?"

When you're curious, you look up someone on social media, maybe scroll through their Facebook or Instagram photos. You pick up the phone or send an email because you want to reignite conversation and be in touch with them *personally*.

Crazy exes do exist, but they're a lot more rare than men would have women believe. It's much more plausible that the woman won't go away because your husband isn't telling her to.

Instead of being worried about her, you need to be worried about your husband's interest in her.

Tell him in no uncertain terms, that he can't continue on with this woman. It's gotta be her or you, his wife, and he can't have both— because that's obviously what he's trying to do. If he can't choose you over his relationship with her, your relationship is already over.

"My new husband and our families are at lunch. His ex walks up to the table, gives fake hugs to my husband and his family. When I'm finally introduced, she gives me a fake smile. I say, "Oh! you are the one who went HAM when you found out we got engaged. Are you okay now?" Everyone gasps, then giggles. Was I dirty to do this?"

Yes. Entirely. You were in your petty and that wasn't pretty. You gave her too much energy by letting her know you still care even though you're the wife.

Living well is the best revenge. She would have been way more in her feelings, which is what you wanted, if you had been gracious and sweet or indifferent. You would have come off perched in your position. Your comment showed your insecurity, and lack of couth in front of your new family. Badly played, ma'am.

CHAPTER EIGHT

What had

happened was...

Whether to stay with a cheater is a question that used to cause me a great deal of conflict to answer. I want to see relationships work, and I acknowledge that people make mistakes. I also know that at least 45 percent of married women cheat, and 50 percent of married men do the same, according to the *Journal of Couple & Relationship Therapy*. You can imagine that the numbers are higher for couples who haven't upped the stakes by vowing fidelity before their God, their family and their friends.

Advising people to leave over cheating means that a whole lot of folk would be packing their stuff. I also hesitated to say that because infidelity is something that can be worked through, if both parties are willing to put in the work.

It became significantly easier to say "Walk!" without hesitation in 2011 after I moderated a relationship panel with six celebrity men at the *Essence* Music Festival. The topic of infidelity came up, of course, and it was TV journalist Jeff Johnson who broke down cheating so it can "forever and consistently be broke". As a self-confessed "reformed cheater", he advised unmarried women who are in relationships *not* to stay when their partner cheats.

His logic went something like this: When an unmarried man cheats, it's a flagrant sign that his partner is not "the one." You are perceived as a placeholder while he looks for her. Unmarried men only cheat on women they do not value, because when they do value a woman, they don't put the relationship in jeopardy. When he finished, the other men on the panel applauded him for keeping it real.

Since then, I've been hyper-aware of patterns surrounding the topic of infidelity. One pattern is that of all the times I'm asked, "D, what do I do about a cheating partner?" it's never a man seeking help.

Of course men get cheated on, and it's devastating to them in much the same way it is for women. But men tend not to want to work it out. There's ego involved, and, too, loyalty consistently ranks among the top three traits that men look for in a partner. Cheating is a huge sign that someone lacks it. Women would do well to acknowledge this, too:

"Should a woman settle for being the 'main' knowing her man has a couple of "side chicks"? That seems to be a popular dating pattern."

God no! It may be "popular", but it's also delusional and one-sided. And messy.

There's nothing wrong with a guy who wants to juggle multiple women... when he's single. That's called dating and carrying on with multiple people sans commitment is entirely permissible. But if he's in a relationship, then he needs to be committed to one person, unless of course the relationship is open, which means each of you are forthright about seeing other people. But in the scenario you describe, this is not the case. He's keeping a small harem and you're expected to be faithful to him.

There's an increased likelihood of catching an STI when a person has multiple sex partners. You're practically begging to catch something signing up for this arrangement.

And let's not even get into the messiness of it all: jealous women calling your phone, you needing "your" man and he doesn't answer because he's with someone else, other women who turn up pregnant by "your" man, etc. Unless you just like drama, so you have a juicy story to tell at the salon, avoid these types of situations, or exit when you discover you're in one.

"My boyfriend and I have been discussing marriage. He says he wants to marry me but doesn't want to be limited to having sex with just one woman forever. He asked me if I would consider parameters for him to mess around, like on his birthday or other special occasions. He doesn't want me to do the same. I'm not totally against it. The exact terms— the frequency of the 'passes,' the consequences for additional violations— are something he and I are trying to work out. Also, I would like to clarify, I'm not that pressed to get married, just simply thinking and discussing what my potential marriage would look like. Does this work for couples ever?"

I'm going to applaud you and your boyfriend for discussing what your expectations are for a marriage *before* you move forward. There's no one way to make a marriage work, and you and your boyfriend are entitled to do your marriage however you like.

However, the glaring issue with what he's proposed is that it is grossly unfair to you. The expectation that you should be committed to him, while he's committed to you on a partial basis, isn't OK. If he gets the "passes" you speak of, you should have a set of your own.

But you don't want any "passes"; you just want him. Whatever your stance is on "passes" or "cheating," do understand that even if you are sexually monogamous, if your partner is not, you're still at risk for sexually transmitted infections, including HIV.

Although everyone likes to focus on the joys of sex, the act can also come with some unintended consequences. You may give your could-be husband a pass to cheat, but how will you know if he uses condoms with his side boo? Are you OK with the possibility of catching a STI, even a curable one? What if it's herpes? What if it's HIV? Are you going to use condoms with your husband to protect yourself from whatever he's exposed to on his "pass" days? How often do you plan to take HIV tests to make sure you're healthy? Will your husband take them regularly, too?

Say that one of his flings gets pregnant. Will you and your husband pay for an abortion? What if she wants to keep the child? Are you going to help him raise the kid? Are you OK with money from your home going to the new child? Will you raise your children with your husband and any children from his mistresses together as one family?

On his birthday and other special days that you're "not totally against" him spending with other women, is it OK if he has celebratory sex with you and then leaves to be with his mistress? How long until you have sex with him after he's back from his "pass"? Immediately? A week? Just curious.

If you've got answers to all these questions and you're fine with these scenarios, I still can't recommend that you take this offer. Despite what you said about not being "that pressed" to get married, it does sound as if you really want to be married, and your desire to become a wife is causing you to overlook some very real and messy consequences of the arrangement he's offered.

"My friend, a girl, thinks that believing any person is capable of being exclusively faithful to one person their whole lives is naïve, unrealistic, and too much to ask. Do you think long-term monogamy is merely aspirational?"

There's a big debate about whether humans are truly capable of being monogamous. The bottomline though is that if you don't think monogamy is for you, that's fine, just don't sign on for the type of relationship where it's expected. And if you are in a relationship and learn you can't stick by the rules (or vows), be honest with your partner *before* you cheat.

"Been with my boyfriend for a year. I read a text that he sent to his former 'friend with benefits' where he told her, "I miss you." I called her, she said that he has denied being with me and he reaches out to her every so often. He tells me that he doesn't care about her and he left her because she caught feelings. Who do I believe?"

My money is on her. You don't send "I miss you" texts to someone you don't care about.

Now about that call you made. Whether you snooped or it popped up on his screen and you saw it, the first and only person you needed to speak with about "your" man is your man. If you can't trust him, you shouldn't be with him. And if he's sending "I miss you" texts to another woman, you shouldn't trust him.

People tend to hate it when I say this. So let me give you another reason not to call the other woman about your man.

As a woman who has been on the receiving end of those calls a couple of times (I wasn't dating either guy), you look plumb crazy asking another woman about your man. In my case, I didn't have a remote interest in either of the men. Now, if I did have an interest, and I was a different kind of woman, those calls would have given me ammunition to go after whom I wanted. Clearly, the relationship is shaky if you're calling another woman to ask about "your" man. She can exploit the wedge between you two for her own benefit.

In your case, he's already sending "I miss you" texts. And to be clear, not "I miss sex with you", but "I miss you", as in *her*. She already has indication that he wants her, you calling means it's more attainable. Don't send that message if you're planning to stay in the relationship.

"I just found out that my fiancé who I've been with for 8 years has been sexting a married woman. I feel so hurt and disrespected, but I'm not sure if there was anything more going on than just sexts. Where do I go from here?"

They're more than likely having sex, just so you know. But let's go with facts: after 8 years, he's exchanging explicit pictures with a woman who's not you. If they haven't had sex yet, that's what the pictures were building up to. They were exchanging them as either a preview or a reminder.

Immediately call off the wedding. You don't marry a man knowing he cheats on you unless you are okay with him doing it throughout your marriage. Marriage doesn't miraculously turn cheating men into faithful husbands. A wedding ceremony isn't a baptism.

Maybe you want to work through this and marry him anyway, but don't limit yourself to a deadline of rebuilding trust. It's a process and there's no set time-frame for how long it will take. And what you don't want to do is be bound to a wedding date and when it rolls around, be unsure of the person you're commit-ting to.

"Do you think a man that has cheated in all his past relationships can suddenly be married and remain faithful? Do you believe once a cheater always a cheater?"

I do believe people can change. But not "suddenly" or overnight for lasting change.

Marriage doesn't make anyone into a different, bet-ter, faithful human just by saying "I do." If he was cheating right until the wedding, he may take off for the honeymoon, but he'll be right back at it as soon as the novelty of the marriage wears off, if it takes that long. (I've read stories of men who have cheated on their honeymoon.)

Another thing, I don't subscribe to the "right wom-an" myth, or that a woman so amazing will come along and then a man who was horrible will suddenly become great. That outlook implies that all the women who came before "the one" deserved to be treated poorly because they weren't good enough. The guy who's a rampant cheater will meet a great woman and cheat on her too because his moral compass is broken and he doesn't respect relationships. He won't become a faithful man unless he works on himself to become one.

"My ex and I broke up a month ago. We were together for four years. He cheated... again. I'm really broken up about it. I've been crying almost everyday I don't know where to go from here. I've been journaling, trying to get it all out but I don't think it's working. What else should I do?"

Forgive him. And forgive yourself for sticking with him and wasting your pretty after the first time he cheated and you chose to stay. You wanted to believe he was better than he was, and he wasn't.

If you're like many women who've been cheated on, you're taking the blame for his actions. You wonder what *you* did wrong and why *you* couldn't keep him. That's a normal reaction, but you're not responsible for what he does. He made a choice to cheat. *Not you.*

It's hard not to care what someone you care about thinks of you. And since he's been cheating, he's made it clear he doesn't value you. Remember this though: *he doesn't get to define your worth.* Because he doesn't see it, and he doesn't respect you, doesn't mean you're worthless or deserving of disrespect. *You are worthy,* no matter how he treated you.

It's been one month. You're on the right track journaling and even crying. Also, do your best to get out of the house and try to have fun even if you don't feel like it.

"When a man tells you the truth about everything, which includes other girls, but he claims he cares about you, is that a good thing or a bad thing because he is not leading you on?"

Honesty is a respectable trait, and when a guy is forthright with you about the dirt that he does, that's great because it gives you the opportunity to make an informed decision about what exactly you're signing up for.

But being honest about his shortcomings doesn't excuse or absolve him of them. He's still acting up; you're just not in the dark about it. And if he's acting up, judge his level of care by *his actions, not his words.* If his actions include other women and he's supposed to be committed to you, he doesn't care all that much.

"I'm married. He's married. We haven't done anything physically, but we are so connected, to the point that we are both willing to leave our respective spouses. Is there a right way of doing this? Am I wrong? I haven't touched

him out of respect for his wife, but I still feel
bad."

It sounds like you're having an emotional affair and
there's no way around it: it's just plain wrong. I appreciate that so far you've kept this illicit relationship
from getting physical, but it's troubling that your motivation is respect for your sort-of-boyfriend's wife,
but not respect for your husband, your marriage or
even yourself. That tells me a lot about your union, this
secondary relationship you've pursued and your self-
esteem. You're in way over your head, and whether or
not you know it, you're about to sink. I'm not so sure
that your partner— the other man, not your husband— will go down with you.

If you've honestly exhausted all efforts to make your
marriage work, then it may be time for you to go. But
running into the arms of the man with whom you've
been emotionally cheating isn't the move you want to
make. Is a man whose own wife shouldn't trust him
really the kind of man you want to call your own?

I need you to understand a couple of important
things about what you're doing, and with whom you
are doing it. Sure, there's a long-shot chance that this
side hustle could pan out into something meaningful
and long-term. Relationships that start from affairs
survive 5 percent of the time, according to psychologist
and talk-show host Dr. Phil.

There's a good reason for that. The foundation of your side relationship is built on lies, deception and dishonesty. If you're cheating— whether it's emotional or physical— you're already demonstrating a lack of the fundamental skills that make healthy relationships most likely to work, the biggest of which is integrity. You and the man with whom you're cheating aren't demonstrating a healthy dose of it.

SECOND CHANCES

"During a group talk about cheating, I say I will not take back a cheating boyfriend. Since then, my boyfriend is mad, saying that if I really loved him, I will at least try to work things out. Then he asked, 'what about loyalty?' Is he feeling guilty?"

I can't tell if he's guilty based on this information, but he is slightly delusional. Not only is he mad about a hypothetical situation, he expects you to continue your loyalty to him without missing a beat, right after he's been disloyal to you. That's laughable. I assure you if the tables were turned and you cheated on him, he would not show you automatic loyalty.

I've said this before, but it can't be repeated enough. Loving someone else is a beautiful thing. But *you have to love you too.* And part of that love isn't sticking by people blindly when they lie to you, deceive you, and put your health at risk by cheating on you.

Your boyfriend wants you to even *consider* sticking around if he cheats? He needs to make you a wife, and there are still no guarantees even then. (Note: the rules about cheating can differ slightly for wives vs. non-wives.)

"My boyfriend and I spent a lot of time together, hanging with friends, meeting family, taking road trips, etc., over the last six months. This week, I found out he's been in a relationship with another woman for 8 or 9 months. He says it was simply for financial reasons. I made him call the girl on three-way, and he told her that he wanted to work on things with me, and that she took their relationship more seriously than he did. My friends and family think he genuinely cares for me, but didn't know how to break things off with her. Do I believe them?"

Your friends and family likely see how happy your boyfriend makes you and they want to continue to see a smile on your face. That's the only reason I can think of for them to give you bad advice.

Your guy isn't what he seems. He may like you, and spend a lot of time with you, and introduce you to people, but he was also in a relationship with someone else when he met you, and he's spent the last six months lying to you by omission about Girlfriend Number One.

Even if he was with her for financial reasons, he was with her. And your friends and family are making illogical leaps to explain that. If he didn't want to be with her, all he had to say was, "I don't want to do this anymore." He opted not to do it. And whether she took the relationship more seriously, it was still a relationship that he was in.

Don't make the mistake of thinking that because he does someone else dirty by using her for money or embarrassing her on the phone, that he also won't do the exact same thing to you someday. He doesn't respect relationships— not the one with her, and not the one with you.

"I recently found out that my boyfriend of almost seven yeas was cheating on me. This isn't the first time. I have forgiven him in the past, but this time I kicked him out of our apartment. Now I am having second thoughts about this and want to attempt to mend the relationship. Do you think it's worth it?"

He's established a pattern of cheating on you. The only way you should consider taking him back is if you're okay with being cheated on going forward. Are you?

I get that you miss him and that he has redeeming qualities that you like. But in order to access those, you have to put up with the side of him that doesn't respect you, that runs around with other women and breaks your heart, too. He's cheated on you twice already. How many more opportunities are you going to give him to do it again?

"My ex lied and cheated throughout our relationship— emotionally and physically. It all came out at the end. He insists he still wants to marry me and work on his commitment issues. Is it his ego or guilt making him want to hold on?"

Maybe both. He likes you. That's why he was in a relationship with you. But he wants to have other options, and he's been exploring them all along behind your back.

I'm sure it's tempting to consider his offer. Even though he's been lying to you all along, you still care about him and a man you probably love is talking about marrying you. You should know that marriage doesn't change people. If he's a philandering boyfriend, he will be a philandering husband.

"Ex and I broke up two years ago because of him cheating and being generally immature. Now he is coming back around claiming to be a changed man. I thought he was The One. Can people really change, or does that only happen in movies (i.e., Big/Carrie)?"

You're asking, if your life were *Sex and the City*, would Mr. Big ever become the guy who loves Carrie (that would be you) and treats her like he should have all along?

Not likely. People can change, of course, but unless there's some life-altering event like a religious conversion, kicking an addiction or getting over a serious illness, your ex isn't likely to have a "road to Damascus" moment. If the breakup and the aftermath didn't result in an "aha moment" that made him realize he had been taking you for granted, your ex is unlikely to do a 180-degree conversion months or years later and become the person you always envisioned he would be.

People grow, mature and get different perspectives on their relationships all the time, but it's usually when they are involved with someone else. The best you can hope for— and don't hold your breath— is an apology for what your ex put you through. That awakening often comes when exes are either in love with someone else who did to them what they did to you or are so blissfully happy that they want to erase their bad karma to keep the new relationship in tip-top condition.

"You must have never been cheated on, which if not, how very fortunate for you. How can a woman just get up and walk away and say "bye-bye" when feelings are involved?"

I never said the choice would be easy. In fact, it won't be. It's hard to leave when you care about someone even when they haven't wronged you, but it's completely feasible.

I would never discount your feelings for someone else, but I'm asking you to consider your feelings *for yourself* and how your partner feels about you, if he's betrayed you, lied to you, deceived you, and put your feelings second to his own. By staying, you're putting someone first who puts you second. And that's not fair *to you*. At some point, you've got the take the man off the pedestal and stop looking out for someone who doesn't do the same for you. You're all into him, he's all into someone else. *Who is looking out for you?*

"People make mistakes. You don't think there's recovery from cheating? Not even if he apologizes sincerely, vows to be a better man, then actively strives toward that? I think it's possible, especially if he wasn't cheating constantly with tons of chicks."

It's possible, but it's extremely hard for a relationship to recover from cheating and be healthy again. But you're right— kind of. It's possible, but only one of the steps on your list has merit. Apologies are nice gestures and so are vows, but they're also just talk, and words don't mean a lot from someone who just got caught cheating.

To move through— not over, not past— cheating, I only recommend that wives who want to work it out put forth the exceptional effort. And my advice for them (in addition to seeing a therapist) is:

1. **Stop having sex for three months.** That's not an arbitrary time frame or a punishment. It is, however, how long it can take for HIV antibodies to show up in test results. You and your partner must get tested for sexually transmitted infections and HIV immediately, and before going forward. If he or she balks, the relationship is a wrap. Your health is more important than any relationship, including a marriage.

2. **Vent (to your partner).** Your partner needs to understand the impact of the infidelity on you and your relationship. It's also time to go over the boundaries of what is acceptable to you and what is not. Make it clear that this is the only chance you're offering. If he cheats again, you're out— for good.

3. **Address the core issue or issues that led to the infidelity. (Otherwise it will happen again.)** That means you're going to have to talk to your partner about what he believes he isn't getting from you and looked elsewhere to find. Does your partner need to feel more appreciated? Is your mate feeling supported?

You'll also likely want to know exactly what happened. This can be a hard conversation. However, if your partner wants to make the relationship work, then he will make the effort. This conversation will also allow you to gauge the level of deceit. If you're on the fence about working it out, knowing the details can help you decide whether it's worth the effort.

Set an ongoing schedule for when the two of you will check in with each other to assess the relationship and address any wants, needs and concerns.

4. Look for action. Your trust has been violated. You need to see action from your partner that he or she is committed and worthy of being trusted again.

5. Forgive. This is a day-by-day process. There's a reason that infidelity is often referred to as something couples "survive," not "get over."

"I heard someone say that a married woman is supposed to forgive the first time her man cheats on her. Do therapy, try to let him do right. Do you believe that marrieds get a 'pass' on one affair?"

There's no "pass" for cheating just because you took vows. And no one with sense blames a woman, married or not, for leaving.

However, I do think once you've pledged "for better or for worse" you owe the union a shot at trying to work things out. You don't just leave your marriage without giving it some very serious thought, unless there's abuse.

He cheats, you *both* need to figure out why and get to the bottom of it. Restoring the trust in the relationship is a long, hurtful, uphill battle. That it's helpful to have a therapist on hand.

Forgiving your partner and even trying to work it out, does not mean you automatically stay in the marriage. You may learn details about your partner's infidelity and his outlook and expectations about the relationship that are not acceptable to you. You may decide as you consider what he's done that you don't want to stay with someone who can so easily deceive you. And that's fine.

"My husband has cheated on me a couple of times. I told him if anything happens ever again, I'm going to divorce him. My heart is broken, and I have nightmares about this chick. I don't know how to trust him. I love him and want it to work, but I don't know how this can be fixed. Do I move on?"

Your husband has cheated two times that you are aware of. Despite his pattern of infidelity, you've decided to stay in a marriage in which both of you are clearly unhappy.

While you very well may mean, "If I catch you a third time, I'm out!", from your husband's point of view, the threat is idle. You didn't leave the first time, and after that incident you probably threatened to go.

You didn't say what, if anything, changed in your relationship afterward, but the core issues were still there if he repeated his behavior.

And when you caught him a second time, you stayed again. The message you're sending him is that you will make a lot of fuss, but when it boils down to it, he can cheat and you're not going anywhere.

Plenty of couples choose to work through infidelity in a marriage, which is their choice. But I'm curious as to what, if anything, you and your husband have done to actually work on the issues in your relationship.

If you want an actual shot at continuing this union without him seeking other women, both of you will have to do some work to get this marriage back in order. I suggest that you consider going to therapy as a couple so you can get beyond issuing threats and actually address the issues. And even then, acknowledging the problems isn't enough—you will both have to change the way you communicate and treat each other if you want to be happily married again.

Notice the emphasis on *both.* Your husband is solely responsible for his cheating. That is not on you. But *both of you are responsible for whatever breakdown there is in the marriage that led to his infidelity.* You and your husband are in this relationship together. It takes two to make a marriage work—and two to make it a mess. Both of you will have to make changes.

"So are you saying if you're in a relationship and your boyfriend cheats leave? And if your husband cheats, get counseling?"

Counseling isn't the end all be all, like you just go to a therapist, and everything is magically better. The therapist is there to help you work through your feelings and consider all your options. Basically, to help you make a decision about what you want to do with a level-head. Going to therapy does not definitively mean things get worked out and the couple decides to stay together.

YOU CHEATED

"How do you tell your significant other that you cheated?"

There's no easy way or right time to 'fess up to something that you know is going to ruin someone's outlook for awhile. Just make it plain, kind of like Steve did in the first *Sex and the City* movie when he told Miranda he cheated on her. "I had sex/kissed/went out with someone else" is sufficient.

"I've been in a relationship for two years, and I guess things got comfortable, and we just stopped trying to make it work. Meanwhile, I met a guy and we've been talking a lot. I think I am falling for him. He says he wants me to leave my boyfriend. How do I get out of this mess? How can I save my relationship or even make a choice?"

You don't want the guy who meets you knowing you have a man and pushes up anyway. He doesn't respect relationships. And to be fair, neither do you. This is a mess waiting to happen.

If you don't want to be in your current relationship anymore, then leave. But leaving one situation, especially for the guy you cheated with, and hopping straight into another relationship doesn't benefit you. You have no time to mentally recover from the previous relationship and will take all the baggage with you to the next relationship, which won't last long.

You get out of this mess, first by telling the side guy, "good-bye." Then you figure out if you want to put the effort into working to improve your current relationship or if you just want to be on your own. It's your life. You have the power to make decisions about what you want or don't.

"I've been married for three years, but there is no spark between us. I've been really tempted to talk to other men who have been pursuing me, and they are well aware of my marital status. Talk some sense into me, please!"

You're looking for green grass in another yard instead of watering your own lawn because it's easier than rebuilding whatever's broken in your marriage.

Do understand, the men who are pursuing you are interested in sex only. They don't care about you and they don't respect a married woman who cheats on her husband. You're a good time. That's it. And a good time isn't worth putting your marriage in jeopardy, and that's what it will be in if you start fooling around with other men.

No one said marriage was supposed to be easy. Figure out what you would like your husband to do to help you put a spark back into your marriage. Is it more sex? More daily affection? More quality time? Whatever it is that you want, pinpoint it and communicate your explicit desires *to your man*. He'll probably convey some wants of his own that aren't being met. You should *both* brainstorm about how you can each have more of what you want in your marriage.

"My partner messed around on me and at first I felt this was a free pass for me to do so too. I even told him so, and he really couldn't say much. But now that I've met someone else to sleep with, I feel terrible. I don't understand why his conscience didn't make him feel the same way."

He's not you, and he doesn't care the same way you did. I understand your thought process, but you're better than this as evidenced by the guilt you feel. Guilt is your mind's way of telling you that you've gone too far.

You wanted to make things even between you and your partner, but what you've done is bring yourself down to his level of trifling.

His cheating wasn't a pass for you to do the same. It was a sign for you to leave. And so you know for future relationships, playing tit-for-tat is a recipe for disaster. Doing that creates a mess, as you've found. And it doesn't make you feel any better, as you've also discovered.

You want to feel better? Collect up your love and your emotional investments and support and time and keep then to yourself until you find someone worthy of them who will appreciate what you bring.

"I'm a married woman, and have gone to lunch with a man 12 years younger the past couple days. We talk a lot about religion, sports, etc. nothing physical. Is this cheating? Disrespectful? My husband shouldn't have a say, considering an affair he had three years ago."

If you have to ask whether your interactions with the opposite sex are crossing the line, then they probably are. And if you don't want to tell your partner about what you're up to, then yes, you're definitely wrong. It sounds as if you might be toying with the idea of an affair—an emotional one for now—as a way to get back at your husband, who actually does get a say in who you date *because he's still your husband.*

When your husband cheated, you forgave him and decided to stay in the marriage. That doesn't give you a pass to cheat. If you want to remain married, address the hurt you've been holding onto all these years, instead of distracting yourself with a younger man or seeking revenge

Let's not pretend with each other. You like the attention, and the novelty of a new face. So you're justifying what is essentially dating someone other than your husband because you're still upset about the affair he had. If you want to remain married, you have to call the younger man and tell him, "We can't be friends anymore" because it is inappropriate and disrespectful to your marriage to carry on with him. And when you get home, tell your husband that you still haven't resolved your feelings about his affair and you want to go to couples therapy to save this marriage.

"I've been in a seemingly monogamous lesbian relationship for 7 years with my beautiful girl friend. We moved to NYC from [fly-over state] last year. I've now cheated on her 5 times with 5 women. Am I overtaken by lust of the women in NY or is there something wrong with me? I love my girlfriend to death."

Then *act* like it. Love is more than a feeling. And whatever you feel, your actions aren't love. Sorry.

NYC doesn't have potions in the air. Just more options and less judgment. You *clearly* want to see other people (because you're seeing *so many* other people). Cut your girlfriend loose so she's not tied to someone who is cheating on her rampantly. Letting her go is an act of love. Having her and all these other folks is just selfish.

"I am having an affair and now the other man is threatening to tell my husband. He has nothing to lose. How do I get out of this without my husband finding out?"

If you're going to cheat while married, you're supposed to follow the rules, the most prominent of which is cheat with other married people because they have the same thing to lose. If you don't want your husband to find out, then you're going to have give in to the demands of your mister. What is it that he wants in order to stay quiet? Ask him.

Also, know that he knows he has you in a tight spot. Just because you give in to whatever he wants this time to not spill the tea, isn't a guarantee that he won't demand more from you down the line. Instead of being held hostage by his demands, it may be better for you to 'fess up to your husband about what's been going on. You're clearly not happy at home, and based on your actions and want to see other people.

HE CHEATED WITH ME

"Guy I was flirting with asked for my number. My friend said he has a GF. Is it my issue to worry about a man's potential significant other or is that his job to consider her? Do I owe her to resist her man?"

You're looking at this the wrong way. You don't owe anything to a woman who you've never met or never knew existed until your friend informed you. That's asking a lot.

But you do owe it to yourself not to date messy men. And the guy who has a girlfriend, but is hitting on you? He's messy. And he doesn't have respect for his relationships. If you were to ever become his girlfriend, he certainly wouldn't think twice about hollering at other women just because he's committed to you.

The old folks also like to say, "how you win 'em, is how you lose 'em." If you get him while he's with another woman, expect to lose him to another one too.

"I get all the reasons to not be a jump-off/ side chick, but considering all the work that goes into a real relationship and that many side chicks are treated really well, is it really all that bad?"

Yes, you're dealing with a man who is a master manipulator. He lies to his girlfriend or wife about where he is, who he is with and what he's doing. He also lies to you. He doesn't suddenly gain a sense of integrity just because you're around.

However great you are treated as a side chick, the woman who is knowingly or unknowingly playing "wifey" gets 10 times better treatment. If you get a trip to Miami, she gets a trip to the South of France. If you get a Louis Vuitton bag, she gets a Birkin. And let's scale that all way back because the average guy doesn't earn enough to trick like that. It's more like "wifey" gets Houston's and you get Red Lobster. She gets Valentine's Day and Christmas, you get the day after. You both get sexually transmitted infections if he catches anything from any of the other numerous women he may possibly have sex with in addition to you and his "main chick."

If you're standards are really low, then playing second to another woman and dealing with a man with no integrity might classify as "really well". I'd encourage you to raise your standards and require a man to make you, not his main, but his *only woman.*

"Three months ago, I slept with an ex who I didn't know had a girlfriend. I still can't help but feel horrible about my actions. He seems to be doing fine, and they are still going strong. I broke it off as soon as I found out about her and told him to keep his commitment. I don't know how to get over this guilt."

Forgive yourself for trusting your ex when you shouldn't have, chalk up your actions to "life happens" and move on with a clean conscience. He intentionally misled you into thinking he was single because he knew you wouldn't have sex with him, if he was in a relationship. He lied to you. You didn't do anything wrong here. Don't carry someone else's guilt for them.

When you did found out the truth, you cut off the relationship and sent him back to his girlfriend because you respect relationships.

"I have heard you say, "If you're not married, you're single." After a bad breakup I think I finally understand what you meant. I recently, met a nice "eligible" guy, but he has a GF. There is flirting and friendly ice cream dates. Things are rocky with him and the GF. Any advice as to how I proceed here?"

Um. You don't. That line was meant to encourage women not to act like wives when they are not *yet* wives. It is not giving a pass to cheat with a guy in a relationship. And that's what you're doing by dating a man with a GF.

Rocky or not, he's not eligible if he's committed to someone else no matter how bad he says the relationship is. And unless you're cool with him stepping out on you when things get rocky, you should not deal with him. He's showing you by his actions what he thinks of monogamy.

"I found out my boyfriend was still seeing his child's mother intimately. He denied it, but I called and asked her. She said she knew about me and they were in a relationship. We talked more and she got angry. She emailed me to say that he cheats often, but she is going to stay. But if she already knew about me, why is she mad?"

Just because she knew about you doesn't mean she wanted to hear from you. She was probably annoyed that you were calling her.

But ma'am, in addition to taking all the wrong actions— you had no business calling his child's mother— you're worried about the wrong person. You found out that "your" man was cheating on you, and instead of confronting him, you're worried about a woman who has made no commitment to you, and who owes you nothing and you're wondering why she's mad? I'm wondering why you're still calling this man "my boyfriend" and if you've spoken to him about this situation since he's the one you're supposed to be in a relationship with.

I'm also wondering if you've been to see a doctor to get tested for sexually transmitted infections since you know for sure your boyfriend is having sex with his child's mother and she just told you that he "cheats often."

"I went on a few dates with a guy. He finally revealed that he has been in a relationship with a girl I know from college. I stopped talking to him, but he keeps reaching out, calling all throughout the day, texting, emailing and even FaceTime. His girlfriend and I share a mutual best friend. Should I tell his girlfriend?"

No, you shouldn't. Nor should you tell your best friend who you know will go tell her. It's asking for drama, which I assure you that you don't need. But if you want him to stop calling you, tell him you're going to call her. He will likely fall back.

Also, you do know that you can block him from calling, texting and FaceTime, right? Blocking him from email is also possible as well. If you don't want to hear from him, you don't have to.

"My friend introduced me to a nice guy, and after several dates, I decided I really like him. But then I received a call from a woman claiming to be his girlfriend and asking me who I was to 'her' man. I confronted him about what happened, and he said it was his 'crazy ex' and she's jealous that he's moving on. He assured me there was nothing to be worried about. Since then I haven't heard from him and I've called multiple times. I don't know what's going on. Could she really be a crazy ex trying to sabotage his relationship with me, or is he really committed to someone else?"

You met what seemed like a great guy. Sometimes it can seem they are hard to come by. It sounds like you want to hold on to the great possibilities of what could have happened between you. But he's not who he presented himself to be— no matter how nice he was or who introduced him to you or how great those first few dates were.

That woman who called you? She isn't some crazy ex (though they do exist, it's far less than the degree to which they are used as scapegoats). Here's how I know: She called you. Crazy exes aren't left alone with unlocked phones. If she was really the crazy ex he claims, he wouldn't be hanging out with her. No, not even for sex.

That he's been ignoring your calls indicates that you are low on his hierarchy of importance. His reasons for being MIA matter less than the bottom line: Even if there is no crazy ex, when he stops picking up the phone, it's like a big blinking light at midnight on the Vegas strip: he's just not that into you.

"Just got a note from a dude's wife (had no idea he was still married). She reached out to me because, in her words, it was "her only option", to get the truth. I haven't seen this guy in weeks as I was not really interested anyway. Do I reach out back to her? Or let him know she called me?"

I would ignore her. It's really unfortunate that she feels reaching out to you is her "only option". Surely, she knows something is going on and her husband isn't giving her answers she can trust, so she has to validate his stories with other women. That's a terribly sad situation.

But that's not your drama to deal with. You respond to the wife, I guarantee you will hear from her again with either follow up questions or accusations. All she's going to do is go back to her husband and say, "I talked to so-and-so and she said..." And you will likely hear from him too.

The wife knows she is in a bad situation, she wants to know how bad, and honestly, I don't see her leaving. This is just an anecdotal observation from hearing so many stories over the years, but the women who call rarely bounce.

"Met a guy while traveling for work and had a one-night stand (not something I usually do).

We had a great time. He told me afterward that he was married. We emailed a bit, but I left it alone. Now he is coming to town for work and asked to have a drink with me. Do I try to be friends or just stay away?"

You're not friends. He's a guy that you were so attracted to that you had sex with him the night you met him, something you don't normally do. And he's also the guy that either outright lied to you about his marital status or he lied by omission.

After he told you he was married, you had no business emailing him. And now that he is coming in town, you have no business meeting up with him. He's already cheated on wife with you and lied to you and is contacting you behind his wife's back. What more does he need to do for you to see he is the kind of man that comes with loads of drama and tons of baggage?

Some women like the idea of being the other woman. It can seem alluring and a little scandalous. They feel a little more self-important, thinking, *here's this man who has this woman, but he can't resist me and he's willing to put his marriage in jeopardy to be with or to see me.*

That's a fantasy. The truth is you're not the woman he's cheated with or attempted to cheat with. You're just one of the ones that said "yes". You can and should do better than this.

CHAPTER NINE

Sharing Spaces

Admittedly, I'm not the biggest fan of long-distance relationships. When friends or clients ask me if they should pursue getting to know a guy who lives out of state— usually someone they met on vacation or at a work conference, occasionally online— I advise them to have fun but not to get too serious.

And I specifically say "a guy" because while I have male clients and readers on Ask.Fm that ask a lot of questions, I've only heard women ask about long distance relationships (LDRs). Sure, guys date long distance, but most don't contemplate doing it with any seriousness unless there are extraordinary circumstances.

The common male refrain I hear for dating distance is the "45-minute rule," meaning that the travel distance between you and him should be under 45 minutes if you want a reasonable expectation of an actual monogamous relationship. This applies even if you're in the same state or even city. There are plenty of New Yorkers who find that seriously dating someone in Harlem is implausible if they live in Brooklyn. (Without a car, it's a hour-plus commute.)

In the best of circumstances, you get to know each other and enter into a relationship while in the same state, and then a job or school takes you somewhere else. A quick note about that: If you're a dating adult and your partner moves out of state and doesn't ask you to come with him or her (unless, of course, that person is going into the military or away to school), then you're missing the red flag being waved at the bleeding bull: you. See the writing on the new driver's license instead of the wall and bow out gracefully.

The second-best circumstance is that you luck up and find someone who has a plethora of frequent-flier miles or has an immediate relative who is a pilot or stewardess, so you can see each other often— and by often I mean at least twice a month. Even in this ideal LDR situation, expecting monogamy is akin to delusion. I know tons of people in committed LDRs, and while they are emotionally bonded to their out-of-town partner, their other parts are often bonding with someone else on the weekends (or weekdays) that their partners aren't around. If long distance is the way you want to go, get on board with the idea of an open relationship.

Maybe I just know shiesty people. Admittedly, folks don't call and write me to say how well their relationships are going, and perhaps the negativity I hear so often from readers and clients taints my perception. I acknowledge that there are people who don't cheat and are loyal, and that some long-distance relationships work and even result in marriages. There's hope for the optimists.

"Any tips on keeping the fire going in a long distance relationship? We already talk every day and do frequent trips?"

Have an End Date: This is built-in when one partner moves for grad school or heads off to "be all she can be." But when it's a move for a job, the time you spend on Skype and phone calls— or traveling— for your relationship can extend (or drag on) forever.

In the beginning it's fun to have an adventure visiting a new city or returning to your old one. But that gets old quick, especially when you have things to do on the weekend— like errands or hanging with local friends— and you're scheduled to be out of town. Living out of a suitcase becomes more bearable when you know it won't go on forever.

Rely on Technology: The only reason I'm not adamantly against LDRs is the existence of Skype, FaceTime, and Tango. The video-calling services are the closest thing to having someone in the room with you.

Get Old-Fashioned, Too: Penmanship be damned, there's nothing like a letter arriving in the mailbox. Since we all tend to be more expressive when we write, it's an opportunity to let the sweet nothings flow. And since scent is such a powerful sense, spritz the paper with the perfume you wore the last time you were together.

Travel Somewhere Else: You'll soon tire of traveling, especially if you're seeing the same city over and over or constantly playing tour guide. Get out of a rut by planning a getaway with your partner to somewhere neither of you has been before, but you're both eager to explore.

"A guy I've been talking to told me he likes me, but doesn't want to date me until we live in the same state. (We are both planning to move to New York soon.) He says he is thinking logically, but I am thinking emotionally. I feel like I am forcing us to date from afar. How do I accept that he likes me?"

Stop trying to date him. He's already told you that's not what he wants and in trying to get your way, you will end up breaking your own heart. In order to make a long distance relationship, or any relationship, work, you have to have two willing people. You and the guy are not on the same page, and you can't will him to think like you.

Oh, and whether he likes you or not is largely irrelevant if he's not committing. I would put this plan on the back burner until or *if* you and he end up in the same city.

"I started dating a guy that lives in another state. I've known him since college. We went out a couple years ago, but it fell off. We're picking back up and he wants to come to visit me. What's considered too early and what are the rules for this visit?"

It's good that he's coming to visit. I like that he's putting his words into action.

If you're not planning to have sex with him, suggest he stay at a hotel or with a friend. Because he's making the effort to travel, you should plan a day of activities – i.e., an all day date— to show him your city and get to know him. Pick up the tab on at least one activity as a "thank you" for him coming. Other than that, have fun.

"How do I go about having a male guest in town, do I put him on the couch? My bed and make a pillow fort? Or wear raggedy panties

under my PJs? I like dude but I have a habit of moving fast with guys and I want to slow down with this one."

You have an admitted habit of moving too fast, so don't tempt fate with a sexy man laid up in your house. He needs to stay in a hotel or to with one of his boys.

Another tip: masturbate before you go out with him to take the edge off.

"My boyfriend of three years lives an hour drive away and doesn't have a car. Lately, he has become very passive. When we do see each other, I initiate and it feels like I am doing the most. I don't feel loved and when I try to talk about it, he acts like the issue is mine. I'm not sure what to do."

Your relationship sounds extremely unbalanced. It also seems that he has lost interest and instead of bailing, he is not participating and waiting for you to break up with him. It takes two people to make a relationship work and it seems you are the only one working here. You've already tried to talk to him about it. Unfortunately, there's not much to do here except read the writing on the wall.

"Would you relocate to another city for a man's job if you weren't married and have been dating for 8 months?"

No. I'm going to hope by "dating" that you mean you are in a relationship, otherwise this shouldn't even be a consideration without a commitment. And even if you are his girlfriend, it still shouldn't be an option.

I get the romantic temptation to abandon all you hold dear to pursue true love, but you should be practical and require an actionable promise of a future together before you quit your job, uproot your life, and move away from your friends and family. If he wants you to move with him, tell him what you require. If he wants you with him, he will make it happen.

CHAPTER TEN

Getting it In

It would be so much easier for all of us if sex came with a manual— when to have it, how to do it well, who to have it with— or not, how often to have it, or how to get more of it from your partner.

Unfortunately, it doesn't. And as a result, women find themselves in precarious predicaments trying to figure out how to manage without getting caught up, bruising his ego, being judged, settling for wack D, catching a sexually transmitted infection and so much more.

"After how long of dating are guys ready to
sleep with you? Would he not like me if I
wanted to wait to marriage?"

Um. He wants to sleep with you before the first date
if he's attracted to you. Doesn't mean y'all should.

He may not want to wait for marriage and that's fine. Don't base your decision on whether to have sex—
or do anything— on whether a guy will like you.
That's walking down an unpaved road to a bad decision.

"After second date with a guy, he keeps inviting me to his house. Is he just trying to f—?
Our third date is Sunday. We have not kissed
yet or anything! Am I giving off the wrong
vibe?"

You obviously don't want to go, so don't go. You're
not obligated to go anywhere just because you're invited. Tell him you aren't comfortable going to his house,
and suggest somewhere inexpensive that he can take
you in case this is a money issue. If he only wants to see
you, if you're going to his house, then yes, it's all about
sex.

Because he may only see you as a sexual interest
does not always mean you're giving off the wrong vibe.
If you want more, and it sounds like you do, cut your
losses.

"I know you don't believe in discussing how many sexual partners you've had with someone you are dating, but what about if you are about to get married? Is that something that should be known— or, if your partner wants to know, should you discuss it?"

I'm not a fan of disclosing your number under any circumstances. For a woman, there is no right answer, and any answer is likely to be used against you. No matter how tame your past may be in comparison with that of the man asking, you're likely to be looked down upon in some way. It's slut-shaming at its finest.

If you have the misfortune to be on the receiving end of this query, you should dodge the question by getting to the heart of what the asker really wants to know by responding to the question with a question: "What is it that you're really trying to determine?"

Usually the inquirer is trying to gauge if you're more sexually experienced than he is, how well (or not) you're likely to perform in bed, the likelihood of you having a sexually transmitted infection or how likely he is to run into someone you've had sex with.

If you're discussing marriage, I'd guess that your fiancé probably knows whether the two of you are sexually compatible. But he may be feeling insecure and wondering how he stacks up against other men. Give him some ego-stroking assurance by insisting, "You're the best, baby." Whether true or not, it's the only sensible answer to give a man.

Occasionally, you may encounter a man who just insists on knowing your number. Recognize it for the mauve flag that it is. He's likely not too enlightened when it comes to what matters in relationships, and once you tire of his badgering and answer the question honestly, he'll probably demonstrate that to you in other archaic and sexist ways. If it gets to that point, run— don't walk— to the nearest relationship exit. Your number isn't his problem. You being a woman is.

"Talking to a man about sex and it was clear that I had more experience than him. He started saying I was a "freak" and it made me feel bad. Do men feel "a way" if they realize a girl is more sexually experienced or open than them?"

Some. Dare I say, most. There's a lot of room for progress when it comes to the way women and men think of women's sexuality. A lot of people still expect women not to have much experience and certainly not to lead in the bedroom— or wherever you like to have your sex. Many people believe it's the man's role to, as Brian McKnight so crassly put it, "show [her] how her [vagina] works."

The guy you were having this conversation with was insecure about his inexperience and to cover that up, he tried to shame you. If you decide to hang out with him, which I don't suggest, certainly do not have sex with him.

"As a woman, how much of a freak in the sheets can you be and still feel you can hold your head up as a respectable woman? I was talking with my girlfriends about this the other day. What are your thoughts?"

You can be an entirely respectable woman and also be a stone cold "freak". They aren't mutually exclusive labels.

If you don't want people knowing your freaky feel-good business, then you and the person you have sex with shouldn't tell folks about it.

"Having sex convo with a group of friends. I admitted that I enjoy oral and anal sex and toe sucking (giving more than receiving). They said they don't do it, and it's only for whores. Now I feel uncomfortable with myself. Should you tell everything that's going on in your relationship to your friends? Should certain things be off-limits?"

Your friends don't need to know about your sex life. Would you want your man going to report back to his boys about you?

Have consensual sex, whatever type gives you and your partner pleasure. The only things that are off-limits are the things you and your partner don't enjoy. You don't need your friends to agree with the sex you like unless you're having it with them.

"My BF is insecure about the size of his penis. I can work with it, but he constantly questions whether or not I'm satisfied. What should I do?"

Give him some ego stroke and tell him how much you enjoy sex with him. Add a little extra "umph" to the noises you make when you're having sex. That may help him temporarily. The issue here really doesn't have to do with you, but you're stuck dealing with it as long as you stay.

Your boyfriend is insecure about his size— I'd bet an ex said something about his penis— and only he can fix this insecurity. Your affirming words may help build his confidence, but the hard work of just being good with what he's got? He's going to have to do that on his own.

"When I'm hurt or angry, I don't want sex with my hubby. Even if I force myself, I don't enjoy it. He can feel it and things just get worse. I wish I could get over myself because I

don't want sex to be a bargaining chip in my marriage. What can I do?"

Stop having sex when you're upset, mad, or hurt. You don't like it and as you've found neither does your husband. Like you pointed out, hurt/angry sex just downgrades a situation from bad to worse.

Sex is emotional for you, obviously. That's fine. Instead of "forcing" yourself to have sex when you're bothered, actually address the issues that are upsetting you and resolve them with your mate, *then* have sex. Tell your husband what the plan is so he's in the loop and can work on the problem with you. It's not just your burden to bear as it's an issue that affects you both.

"I love sex and all the kinky, freaky, nasty things that come with that. If I give this to my boyfriend, is it what they say about 'why buy the cow when he can get the milk for free?' Should I save something for marriage?"

I get your logic, but it's slightly off. Great/kinky sex won't get you into a relationship, but it's a bonus in a solid relationship. And while it's not the deciding factor when a guy thinks about proposing, good sex with a great woman sweetens the deal.

Have the sex that you want and that makes you and your partner feel great. If you want to save something for marriage, so you feel like your husband gets something exclusive, so be it. And if you don't do that, that's fine too.

"I hate giving blow jobs but my man loves it. Do you recommend giving blow jobs to keep a man?"

Funny thing: the right man, who treats you the way you want to be treated and pleasures you the right way? He can inspire you to want to do that and a whole lot more. Not to keep him, but because you get pleasure out of pleasing him.

Perform oral sex because you want to, not out of fear of losing your man or obligation. Half of the pleasure in receiving oral sex is having a partner who is willing and enthusiastic about it. And there's no type of sex that will "keep" a man. He might stay around longer, but he won't stay for good just because of sext.

VIRGINS/ CELIBACY

"I believe that I love deeply, yet carefully and I'm yet to get that same love in return. Guys never really put up a fight for me no matter how much I respect and love them and myself. I've held onto my faith and virginity, but I still deal with rejection and loneliness regularly. Why?"

Virginity isn't a guarantee against heartbreak, and it's not really desirable amongst the vast majority of the adult dating population. Most guys you encounter want to have sex.

That's not to say, "have sex now!" That's not a guarantee of a relationship either. You should be true to your faith/beliefs and continue to look for someone who respects your outlook. The goal isn't to have just any man to say you have one. It's to have one that gets you and respects your values. Keep looking.

"I'm an almost 30-year-old virgin who doesn't plan to have sex before marriage, but I still struggle with how to tell potential boyfriends about it. I never get it quite right. I'm always worried about their response. Do you share on a date, after months of dating, etc.?"

The first time a conversation about sex comes up, be honest that you have not had it. Don't announce it like a death sentence. Just a breezy, "Actually, I've never had sex."

It's entirely understandable that you worry about the response. You fear rejection from someone that you like. But the sooner you know whether you and the man you're seeing are on the same page, the better. It's less time emotionally invested and less pretty wasted on a guy who isn't willing to wait with/for you.

"I have decided celibacy is best for me now, at least until I am married or at least in a com-

mitted relationship. Do you think this will affect my chance to get into a relationship?"

Inevitably, when a man and a woman are around each other long enough, the topic of sex comes up. When it does, let him know what you require in order to have sex. It's not that you're not having sex *ever*; it's that you want to get to know him and be in a committed relationship before you have sex. You're not really asking for anything exceptional here. You're a woman, not a Chevy. There's no need for some guy to test-drive you just to call you his girlfriend.

That said, many folks will make you think you're crazy for not having sex. Put this in perspective: There are a lot of women who are having sex— swing-from-the-chandelier, they-only-do-that-in-pornos kind of sex— and they are just as single as you are. Sex doesn't guarantee you any sort of relationship, much less a marriage.

I will also advise you to really stick to your guns on this one. If you're going to tell a man, "X is my requirement," then you need to hold to your word so that you're taken seriously. For clarity, that means standing firm even when he's really cute and super nice with a broad back and wide thighs. It's easy to be celibate when you're not attracted to someone; it's much harder when you are. Try investing in a good vibrator to keep your totally healthy and completely natural urges in check. It still counts as celibacy when you take care of yourself.

"I've been celibate for almost five years. Yeah, I know— 'Man down! Code 10!' I am trying to wait until I am married to have sex again, but it's becoming extremely hard. My male and female friends tell me to just 'get it in,' but I follow a male relationship expert, and he says, 'Wait until marriage.' Is it ever OK for a woman to just 'get it in' with no strings attached and still be considered a lady and not a 'ho'? I don't want a list of men, but this celibacy thing is wearing me down, especially since I haven't had a date since Moses parted the Red Sea. Sigh."

If you want to "get it in" with no strings attached, then that's your business. You can be called a "ho" whether you've had sex with one person or 100. The label, one largely applied only to women, is about controlling your sexuality, not a genuine concern for your well-being or soul.

You're wondering what people will say if they find out. I'm wondering why you are telling others about what goes on in your bedroom or who goes in there with you. It's none of their business.

As for your current celibacy, I don't know whether to congratulate you or console you. It's fine not to have sex, even if it seems as if everybody else is doing it. But it seems that you're sticking to this choice because of the rantings of an arbitrary male relationship expert and because you don't want to be judged by society's double standard about women who have sex. Those aren't good reasons to be celibate.

I'm less concerned about what the relationship expert thinks and more concerned about what *you* think. Do you think you'll regret it or feel guilty if you have sex? Then don't do it. If you think you'll be just fine, do it. It's your body. You can do what you want *or not* with it, as long as it isn't harming anyone else.

If you give it some thought and decide that you do want to remain celibate, I suggest that you join a support group like Worth the Wait Revolution, where you'll find like-minded women (and men) who are also waiting for marriage to have sex and will support you in your struggle to stick to your beliefs, which clearly isn't so easy.

Also, I know your friends like to tease you about your decision, but have a heart-to-heart with them about being more supportive of your choice. Celibacy is a really hard decision, and it's so much worse when you're being dragged for your choices.

Whatever you decide, I recommend that you set up an account on an online dating site for the obvious reason that you can begin dating again. I find that a lot of celibate women who are waiting until marriage to have sex are not actively dating, which makes me wonder how they ever expect to find a husband to have sex with.

"Could it be dangerous to marry someone before having sex and risk the chance of being sexually incompatible?"

If sexual compatibility is important to you and having sex before marriage doesn't go against your core values, then have it before you get married so you know what you're in for. Sex isn't everything, but it is a big thing in relationships. In fact, it's one of the top two issues that couples argue about (money is the other one.) If you know that you're in sync sexually, it's one less thing you have to worry about after you're married (at least for awhile. In sync couples can fall out of sync.)

If sex before marriage falls outside of your value system, then you need to have in-depth conversations about your desires and expectations before you're married, and hope your partner sticks to his/her word. If that's not the case after you've taken vows, you're both going to have to put in the effort to get on track and please one another. It can be difficult, but it's totally possible.

"Back with BF after 4 year break up due to distance. Prior to getting back together, I decided I was going to abstain from sex until

marriage for religious reasons. We slipped up, but now I am stronger in my resolve to wait. He understands, but is not happy. Otherwise our relationship is perfect. We plan to marry next year. What to do?"

You did the right thing being upfront about your new outlook. You told him your terms and he accepted them.

Don't be too hard on yourself for slipping up. Sexual desire is healthy and natural and it is very hard to abstain, as you know, and especially when you're around someone you're attracted to.

Your boyfriend is probably annoyed by what comes across as wishy-washiness. You told him you don't want to have sex until marriage, but for circumstances *on your terms*, you've shown that you will have it before then. You've said your resolve is strong, but your previous actions have said, and louder, otherwise.

I have a male friend who is in a similar situation as your boyfriend. His girlfriend wants to wait for marriage and as he expects to marry her, so he is fine what that. What drives him nuts are her mixed signals. She says she doesn't want to have sex, but she makes a habit of straddling him and grinding on him. He understands and respects that though she doesn't want to have sex, she does want to be sexual and sexy. But he's very frustrated by it.

I suggest you and your boyfriend have a conversation about what the limits are in your relationship. Also, if you're both ready for marriage, consider moving the date up so you can both have the sex you both clearly want and without *you* feeling morally compromised.

"My ex and I were having sex for all of our 2 year relationship, but once I decided to stop it was a BIG deal to him. I made this decision to get more out of our relationship in other ways, but he doesn't understand that. I feel like I've wasted a two-year investment. Is sex really that big of a deal?"

Yes!!!! Sex is not everything, but it is a BIG deal. Very big.

It's one thing to tell your partner going into the relationship, that sex isn't an option. But two years into the relationship, you changed the terms of the agreement by making a unilateral decision to exclude a major part of the relationship. That's a huge problem.

I don't know what you were hoping to improve by removing sex, but if you're now on the brink of a break up, I would say it's clear you've taken the wrong approach. If you want to salvage this "investment", how about instead of punishing your partner— because that's what removing sex from the relationship feels like to him— you tell him what you feel is missing and together, brainstorm ways to fill that void?

Also, I'd like to make one thing clear: you're entitled to do whatever you want— or not— with your body. But that does come with consequences, including the likely end of your relationship.

"I feel like an outcast for not being a fan of casual sex. People think I'm crazy for only reserving sex for committed relationships. Any advice for dealing?"

You deal with the consequences of your actions, and you alone have to look in the mirror and like who you see. Do what works best for you and your body and your sanity. It's okay to be "an outcast" and to go against the grain, especially when what the majority seems to be doing isn't what you want to do.

One tip: if you don't want people commenting on your sex life, don't tell them about it.

"Having morals and realistic expectations seem to be man repellant. Why does it seem like "hos be winning". Serious question."

Here's the big problem with that phrase: the *women* are being judged solely on the perception that they have loose morals— a standard to which men are not usually held. But even if you believe that these women practice less-than-ladylike behavior, that's not all they bring to the table.

What many women who have been called "hoes" have in common is that they are exceptionally attractive. That's a trait that some men— and women— prize. It allows for some people to ignore other potential shortcomings, at least until they get bored. Also, if a woman actually was that sexist epithet, that would not negate any other positive traits she may possess, such as loyalty, kindness or empathy.

Let me also address the very limited definition of "winning" in this case. Because a man has some cash or a degree doesn't mean he brings anything more to the table than money and book sense. Many of us have a bad habit of equating wealth with good character. Money doesn't make anyone a good person. That's not to say that the men in question are bad; just that we should not judge their "goodness" solely on their finances.

STEP YOUR GAME UP

"This is a weird question, but how do I get better at sex? My boyfriend is much older than me and way more experienced. I don't have any complaints about him, and he hasn't said anything, but I get the feeling that it's just OK. I want our sex life to be great. I tried to watch porn to get some ideas and new tech-

niques, but it turns me off. Is there any way to get better at sex?"

In a survey for CommitmentNow.com, 52 percent of Americans reported that they were unhappy with their sex lives. I hope they, like you, are being proactive in addressing that concern.

Start by communicating with your partner that you want to step up your game when it comes to sex. There's an implicit promise there that you're willing to have more sex and try new things, which should go over marvelously.

Before you rush to the bedroom, talk to *each other* about your likes and dislikes and fantasies that you would like each other to fulfill. Remember to keep the conversation positive: "I really like it when you do X" or "Y drives me wild" will go over better than "I hate it when you do XYZ." This is an opportunity for improvement, not criticism. Things may not sky rocket immediately, but a willingness to please is half the battle. Keep up the practice and the enthusiasm, and you'll have your ideal sex life sooner than later.

Ask your partner to be explicitly vocal about what he likes so you'll have cues about what works best for him. Use his verbal cues to figure out what he enjoys the most, and whatever that is, do it more often and with more enthusiasm. Ask him to take the same approach with you.

There's also an option that seems to baffle some people when I suggest it: Take a sex class. Many stores that sell sexual enhancement tools offer instruction on how to improve your sex life. For anything else that people don't know, seeking instruction is a logical step, but when it comes to sex, some find it taboo. It shouldn't be.

"My BF & I like to talk dirty in the bedroom, but it's hard for me to reciprocate. Any suggestions?"

Start light-dirty and work up to nasty-dirty as you're inspired and as he puts it down.

Dirty talk 101:

"Do you like it when I [describe what you're doing/want to do]?"

"I like it when you [*explicitly* describe what you like)]."

"I want you to [*explicitly* describe what you want]."

"[Insert verb] my [explicit name for a sexual body part]!"

"Your [explicit name for sexual body part] feels so [insert *positive* adjective]."

"My husband is working overseas on business for several more months. He keeps asking me to make a sex tape. I am afraid he will either

show it to his friends or lose control of it, but I don't want to be unsupportive. What should I do?"

Usually when I'm asked by women— guys have never asked— about whether to make a sex tape or take nude pictures for their partner, the concern is that if they don't meet his sexual needs, he will get them met elsewhere.

I point this out because it's unusual that your immediate concern is that your husband will share your tape with others. It makes me wonder if you and your husband have had issues with boundaries or oversharing in the past.

Given your concerns, don't make the tape. You're obviously uncomfortable with the idea. Tell your husband that you share his desires for sexual stimulation as much as he does because you and he are in identical situations, but you're just not comfortable making the tape for your stated (and very valid) reasons.

So that you're not just shutting him down, offer an alternative, such as phone sex (or more phone sex than you're having now) and/or sending a care package of sexual goodies that make self-stimulation more pleasurable for him, maybe while you're having phone sex? Consider adding an item of sexy clothing that carries your scent in the very special delivery. Also, if you have the disposable income and vacation time, offer to fly over for a weekend visit so that you can spend time together and have actual, real sex, which trumps phone calls and tapes any day.

"My boyfriend wants me to send him sexy pictures, and I'm hesitant about it. Aside from the fear of them somehow getting out and ruining my hypothetical chances of running for Congress, I'm no Victoria's Secret model! With all these naked picture scandals, are women still sending their men sexy pictures?"

The advent of email and camera phones means that going forth, people will forever and always send naked pictures to their partners. I wrote an article about this subject for the October 2014 issue of *Essence* magazine and in my research I found that 1 in 5 Americans with a smart phone sext (i.e., send sexy pictures to their partner), according to a Harris Interactive poll, and the same poll found that 11 percent of Americans say they record explicit videos on their phones. Lots of those images will be seen by people for whom they were not intended.

You're right to be concerned about your pictures getting out. There's a growing phenomenon of "revenge porn," in which disgruntled (and sadistic) exes, including husbands, post photos and tapes of their former partners online. No woman thinks this will happen to her until it does. You seem to be the rare exception. Kudos for that!

I suggest that you tell your boyfriend "no". If he needs a visual, invite him to come by and have a long look at you. He can even touch, which will make it more fun for both of you.

If you still decide to send him pictures, don't worry so much about your body. If he's asking for photos, you can be reasonably confident that he likes what he sees. But make sure you take pictures the smart way. That means your face and any other identifying details like tattoos, scars, hair or unique backgrounds shouldn't be in the shot. Also, keep it classy. It's more titillating for your partner to see you completely naked, bent over or spread-eagle, but the goal of your pictures should be to ignite a desire for him to show up in person to see more of you.

FRIENDS WITH BENEFITS

I'm an advocate of a single woman getting hers, even sans a relationship. Women have desires, too, and as far as casual sex and health go, it's far better to have one partner fulfilling your wants and needs than several. That said, if you're grown enough to play adult games, you also need to be ready to play by the rules of them.

"I have a male friend with benefits/jump off that I actually like beyond the sex. I admire this man's hustle, work ethic, goals, etc. How

do I go about pursuing a more serious relationship with him? I have read your [first]
book and understand what may or may not result from this, but the answer is always "no"
until you ask. Just curious to know where I
should start and what I should say if I decide
to pursue something more with him."

To ask about a relationship at this point is setting
yourself up for a great likelihood of rejection, perhaps
the most-often expressed fear of my lady clients. But to
hear "no" (or its equivalent) won't kill you, even if the
sting of pride in your chest might make you feel that
way.

Since you've read *A Belle in Brooklyn: The Go-to
Girl for Advice on Living Your Best Single Life*, you
know I talk about the rules for casual sex in "A Good
Jump Off Is Hard to Find." Rule No. 6 is "JOs don't
grow into more. So if you want more than sex up front,
don't think sex is the way to get to that "more" point."

Allow me to explain the logic. Say you have a friend
who gets a job managing a new club, the hottest spot in
your town. It's a classy place where entry is only at the
doorman's discretion. When you arrive, you're escorted
to VIP and you can swill rosé like Rick Ross anytime
you desire. This goes on for months, but then one day
you show up expecting the all-access you've become
accustomed to. You text your friend to say you're outside and he tells you, "Sorry, $20 at the door."

You're confused. You've been used to the hook up and suddenly you're expected to pay?! Heck no, you aren't going to wait in a long line, much less pay to go where you've been going for free. Off principle, you will drive to another venue, wait to get inside, buy overpriced drinks at the bar and complain to the bartender about the nerve of that first place that really isn't all that, anyway.

Your friend with benefits is going to think along the same lines when you start talking about a relationship. You've allowed him all access to a valued benefit of a relationship without requiring any sort of effort or commitment up front. *Now* you want him to put forth effort?! He'd rather drive across town to someone else and do that.

"I asked my FWB about actually dating and he said right now he doesn't want to. I'm like "cool, but from now on, I'll just come here, do what we do and leave." He's upset now. But why pretend we're something when we aren't?"

He doesn't want you for more than sex, but he does want you to want him. That's not interest, *it's ego.* The sooner you can distinguish between the two, the easier your life will get—in and out of the bedroom.

"FWB I am physical with. Men I date, I am not physical with. I prefer to not be intimate with someone I'm dating until we are in a committed relationship, and a relationship is not what I expect from a FWB. Is this cloudy judgment or clear thinking?"

Eh... it's a popular outlook. Most women know that despite what some men say, many do judge a woman if she has sex "too soon". Women also know that sex "too soon" in a relationship can often make it complicated and emotionally messy. So they wait to have sex with a guy they want to build with, and have sex on the side with someone whom they really don't care is judging them.

This only becomes an issue when the guy you're actually dating finds out. His thinking is, "why am I wining and dining and putting in work and this other guy is getting the benefits that I want?" The guy you're into feels used.

You only owe your date insight into your sex life if you're having sex with him. If you choose sex with the date, stop having sex with the other guy, and get tested with each new partner.

"Is it fair to ask a man to only be sexually involved with me? I'm in situation where this guy and I really like each other, but I'm not ready for a relationship. I don't mess with anyone else and I don't want to give him up for other women to have. Is that selfish?"

Health-wise, it makes sense to only have one partner at a time. Having concurrent partners is a leading cause of spreading sexually transmitted infections. And while asking someone you're having sex with to be exclusive is sensible, it is unfair to expect it. Exclusivity is a benefit of relationships.

One of the reasons that people don't commit is so that they aren't tied down to anyone and can do what and whom they want without being accountable to anyone else. If you want a reasonable expectation of sexual exclusivity, you need a boyfriend or a husband.

If you opt to have sex outside of a monogamous relationship, my hope here is that everyone is using condoms *and* using them correctly *and* getting tested regularly. But given that there are 20 million Americans newly infected with sexually transmitted infections every year and there are more than 110 million American living with them, according to the Centers for Disease Control, that's doubtful.

ASSAULT

"I was sexually assaulted by a guy I've been dating for the past three months. We had sex once, but he wanted to do a round 2 without a condom, which I expressed to him I didn't want. He kept pinning me down and trying to force himself on me. I got away, but I'm still freaked out. I'm taking steps to try and get past what happened. My friends are trying to convince me that it's not my fault, but it feels like it is anyway. I can't afford a therapist. Advice?"

Unfortunately, your story is common. Nearly 20 percent of American women are raped at some point, according to the Centers for Disease Control and Prevention. Like you, most of these women know their attackers. But having a relationship of any sort— intimate, social, professional, etc.— is not giving consent to have sex.

Nothing about this assault is your fault. It doesn't matter that you said "yes" to the first round— only that you said no to the second and he ignored your protests. He is solely responsible for his own actions, and what he did is a criminal act. You should report him to the police.

What you're feeling— the self-blame and likely self-doubt— is a natural response to what you've been through. It's a lot to carry, and there's no need to attempt to do it alone. I'm glad that you've opened up to your friends about surviving an assault and that they are being supportive. But what you need is a trained professional who can help you sort through your feelings.

Since you can't afford a therapist, call to the National Sexual Assault Hotline at 1-800-656-HOPE, which has more than one thousand trained volunteers available to help. The call is anonymous and confidential unless you choose to share identifying information.

"I am afraid to tell my boyfriend about my past. I was raped when I was in high school by someone I knew, and I don't think I've ever really gotten over it. I think about it sometimes when I'm intimate with my boyfriend, and then I don't want to have sex anymore. This has been a problem in previous relationships as well. I know he's getting frustrated with me, and I know I should say something, but I don't know how. I'm afraid he'll think I am making excuses. I love him and don't want him to leave me because of this. I don't know what to do to fix the problem."

I am incredibly sorry for what happened to you. Catch that wording: "what happened to you." I can tell that you hold a great deal of guilt and shame about being violated, which is entirely normal, you are not responsible for being attacked; that was solely the responsibility of your attacker.

The only way to "fix the problem," as you put it, is to seek therapy. For most women, rape is not something that they can get thru by letting time pass. The emotional trauma needs to be addressed head-on with the assistance of a trained professional. If you're unsure where to start, try the Rape, Abuse and Incest National Network. The good folks there can direct you to a therapist in your area for individual or group counseling.

My first concern is getting you healthy *for you*, but understandably, you want to get better to maintain your relationship. I encourage you to be honest with your boyfriend about what you experienced. He doesn't understand your reaction to sex and is likely feeling rejected. He may even suspect that you are cheating.

The best way to tell him is just to make it plain. Catch him face-to-face when he's not too busy and say, "There's something I need to tell you," and spill. Explain to him that's why you react the way you do when you are intimate with him.

You will probably be surprised at his reaction, which, if he's a halfway decent guy, won't be rejection. He may become angry, a sort of protective reaction, and he may start sharing stories of women from his past who have also told him about similar ordeals.

Trust your boyfriend, whom you obviously really care about, to be a good guy and accept you— all of you— including the good, bad and traumatized. Allow him a chance to really know all of you and support you, too, as you finally address the pain you've been carrying.

"I was raped at 17. I'm now 27 and as a result, I'm a little frigid as far as sex goes. My fiancé loves it rough and when I refuse, he often tells me 'what one woman won't do another one will.' How do I go about letting him know, 'yes, I love making love with you, but the rough stuff makes me [uncomfortable]'?"

You can't. Your fiancé's an a— hole. At the point where he's threatening to cheat on you when you won't do what he wants, he doesn't have much respect for you. He's trying to control you so you'll let him have way. And knowing that you don't enjoy the type of sex he wants and trying to force it on you repeatedly, says, even more about how little he thinks of you. He's not the type of guy you marry.

SAFE SEX

"Is unsafe sex a sign of commitment or a milestone for couples? Aside from it feeling better bare, does it hold any significance in a relationship?"

Hopefully, it means you've been tested for sexually transmitted infections, including HIV, and you are both monogamous, safe *and* have decided to use another means of birth control unless you're trying to get pregnant.

The only advanced commitment it's a sign of is an unrealized agreement to have a child or gamble with your health. If you're not ready for a kid, I hope you're on birth control. And again, *both* have been tested.

"I made the mistake of having condomless sex early on with my boyfriend. Lately, he has been texting his close friend all day and calling her a lot. I no longer trust him and want condom sex. He says, "no" because he's 38 and in a monogamous relationship with me. Not sure how to handle this."

Tell hem flatly "no". If you actually decide to have sex with him, it's a condom or nothing. He will deal.

And really it should be nothing. You think he is cheating on you because he is spending all this time chatting with a "friend". Having him put on a condom is better than nothing, but doesn't solve the problem. You also need to address your suspicions of his infidelity and clear up what's going on.

You don't want to rock the boat too much, I get it. But I want you to be/stay/remain healthy. And if you're having sex with a man whom you believe isn't monogamous, you're putting your health in jeopardy.

"Do you think birth control lies solely on the woman or both parties involved? Sometimes I forget to take my pill and my boyfriend gets mad. Yet he refuses to use a condom. His reasoning is men can't get pregnant, so it's up me

to not let it happen. Our relationship is perfect except this reoccurring fight."

The responsibility of birth control falls on the two
people having sex who don't wish to create a child. If
he wants to ensure you don't get pregnant, he needs to
wear a condom, especially as you forget to take your
birth control pills, making them unreliable in prevent-
ing pregnancy

If you miss your pill and he's not willing to wear a
condom, don't have sex. You getting pregnant when
that's not your goal is not worth the good feeling or his
ego. And just so we're clear, you're practically begging
to get pregnant if you're having sex and missing pills
and not using another means of preventive contraception.

"My boyfriend has violated to the 10th degree.
The other day we were talking about having
kids. I want to wait until we are done with
school and married. He wants kids now. At the
end of the convo he jokes, 'it's ok, I know
where you keep the sewing kit.' I'm like 'huh?'
He then makes a popping gesture as if to imply he's going to purposely damage the condoms. We got into a heated argument because
I don't find it funny to joke about impregnating someone against their will. I told him the
next time we have sex, I need to inspect the

condom myself. He says I'm blowing things up, he was just joking and wouldn't actually do that. We have made up and today we got hot and heavy. I reach into the side table drawer. No condoms. He has hidden them and won't tell me where..."

When a partner prevents access to birth control, it falls under the category of sexual abuse, which is a type of domestic violence.

Unless you want to get pregnant soon, you need to stop having sex with him. It's progressing from a not funny joke (words) to hiding contraception (actions). He wants children now and he is CLEARLY planning to get you pregnant based on his actions.

The reader followed up to ask:

"I didn't know men catch baby fever too. Do you think I should get on some kind of birth control and maybe revisit our discussion about waiting?"

You should not have sex with someone who will ignore your wishes and actively try to impregnate you when he *knows* you don't want to have children.

If you insist on having sex with him, *yes, absolutely,* you should get on birth control. But birth control doesn't ignore the core issue, which is your boyfriend has no respect for your body, goals, perspective, etc.

And *yes*, a lot of men have baby fever. That doesn't give a man the right to poke holes in condoms or hide condoms when he wants to get you pregnant.

"Guy tells me that he prefers not to wear condoms because he gets soft with them. He also doesn't like to pull out. This is a red flag, right?"

Absolutely! No condom, no sex, even if he did pull out. It's unfortunate that he doesn't stay erect with a condom on. That's something he's going to have to deal with. You, however, will have no parts of this.

Your health trumps his sexual dysfunction, and if he's accustomed to having sex sans condom and not pulling out, I assure you the condom isn't his only issue. His stated M.O. should let you know he's very familiar with sexually transmitted infections, and has multiple children with different women and/or he's paid for several abortions. He doesn't need to have sex again until he is married.

"I have herpes and am sexually active. I rarely have an outbreak. If I am having one, I have no sexual contact. Even when I'm not having one, I don't allow men to perform oral sex on me. Do I still need to tell every casual partner I have it, if we use condoms and no oral?"

Absolutely. I'm guessing when you contracted herpes, the person who gave it to you didn't have an outbreak either. Otherwise, you wouldn't have had sex.

The tricky thing about herpes is that it is most commonly passed on through a process called "shedding" that occurs just before you have an outbreak and doesn't have any visible signs, according to the Centers for Disease Control. That means that even when you're not having an outbreak, you can still infect your partner with the virus.

Talking about your sexual transmitted infection with a potential partner will be uncomfortable. However, the awkwardness doesn't negate the necessity of being upfront and allowing your partner to make an informed decision about having sex with you. You MUST have this conversation with every partner *before* you have sex.

Whenever the conversation about sex comes up, as it always inevitably does, be straight up with your partner about your sexually transmitted infection. This information goes over significantly better if you don't announce it like a confession and just make it plain: "I contracted herpes from a previous relationship. I wanted to inform you upfront." Tell your potential partner how you manage the infection and encourage him to research it as well.

"I am ready to have sex with a guy I am dating, and I want to do the right thing and get
tested [for HIV] first. I don't know how to
bring it up though. I tried to discuss getting
tested with a man I dated before him. He
flipped and said he didn't need to be tested
and it was like I was telling him that I didn't
trust him. How can I avoid this happening
again?"

First: I am proud of you for putting your health
first. Second: The guy who flipped out is a statistical
anomaly. According to the CDC, Black folk are "more
likely than other races and ethnicities to report that
they have been tested for HIV at least once—65 percent versus 46 percent for Hispanics/Latinos and 41
percent for whites."

There are a couple of reasons he could have had
that reaction with you. One, he's not comfortable with
the idea of getting tested. Maybe he's engaged in risky
behaviors, and he could be afraid of what the test results would show. Despite what he said about not needing to get tested, if he's been sexually active, he does.
Two, saying you don't trust him was a weak way of
dodging the issue at hand.

Getting tested obviously can be a touchy topic for
some people. Next time there's a conversation about
sex with the new guy—because there's always a conversation—casually suggest that the two of you "get

tested together." *Together* is the key word. You want to know his current status, and he should want to know yours as well. Hopefully, he's on board—if he isn't, sex is not an option—but "just" agreeing to the idea is not enough. Plan a date and time, again, *together.*

If you just have a preference to go to a doctor's office or a free testing site, that's fine. But you and your partner can also test yourselves conveniently and accurately using an at home testing kit, the same ones used in medical offices, and know your status in minutes. Once you both have your results—hopefully, negative—you can "celebrate" right then and there.

"Guy I'm seeing brought up the "I'm ready to have sex" talk. I brought up getting tested. He balked at the idea and has been funny all week. Sex talk fell back. Should I just dead it?"

I'm afraid of people who don't know the status of their sexual health, and are unwilling to find out. It makes me wonder what risky behaviors they have been engaging in that they don't want to know the consequences of. It's terribly irresponsible. If you are grown enough to have sex, you need to be grown enough to protect yourself and your partner. And you can't do that to the fullest extent if you are having sex and unwilling to get tested regularly.

If he's not willing to come around and get tested, he doesn't need to be talking about sex, and certainly not having it. The appropriate next step is to end this situation.

"BF hadn't had sex in years and went raw. We did not get tested before sex. I asked him later about getting tested and he said he trusted me enough and that he did his part to not get me pregnant by pulling out. My period is on now, but I'm still fearful of an STI. I can't talk to him."

If you really can't talk to your boyfriend about your concerns about sex or anything else, you don't need to be in a relationship, and certainly not having sex. Being able to communicate with your partner and have difficult conversations is a part of a healthy relationship.

You *can* talk to him, you are just scared of how he may react. You have to face your fear and have a conversation about your sexual health. Your health is more important than any other fear you face.

Your boyfriend's answer to your query isn't sufficient. He isn't informed about his sexual health and trust does not prevent sexually transmitted infections any more than pulling out guarantees you won't get pregnant. You both need to be tested for STIs immediately so you're *both* aware of your health status.

Tell your partner that despite the previous conversation, you're still very concerned about your own and his sexual health, and you want to get tested for sexually transmitted infections *together*. If he balks, insist. And if he still refuses, you get tested and you don't continue to have sex with him. Your health is more important than having sex, and a having a man too.

"I love and trust my boyfriend, however, I love myself more and need to look out for me. Should couples continue to get tested during the course of their relationship, and if so, how often? How can I explain additional testing since we're monogamous?"

Yes, monogamous couples should continue to be tested. The truth is, as much you trust your partner, you're only 100 percent sure about what you do. There have been several stories about married women who have contracted HIV from their husbands who were not faithful.

Admittedly, getting tested when you're in a monogamous relationship can be tricky to explain. Some partners will take it as an indication that you don't trust them or that you have put yourself at risk by stepping out of the relationship. In general, I don't condone lying, but I make an exception here: tell your partner that your doctor recommended you get tested annually, which is the recommendation of most doctors. Then insist that he follow the doctor's orders along with you.

SEXUALLY UNSATISFIED

"I'm in a 2-year relationship. My partner doesn't sexually please me. We've communicated about it, and both made efforts to improve, but still, no satisfaction. I love him. Now what?"

Now you can keep trying to work with him to get on the same page, as frustrating as that is, *or* you can accept that you're not going to be sexually satisfied. *Or* you can call the relationship a wrap.

Sex is not everything, but it is a BIG deal, as I've written before. And I want women to feel entitled to sexual pleasure in the same way that men do. Men have no problem expecting to be satisfied and pleasured. Women should feel the same. Life is too short to have bad sex.

"I've been dating a guy for almost a year. We had our first sexual encounter last night. He is horrible in bed and is bad at performing sexual favors. I even faked it a few times. He is a sweet guy and this is his only flaw. I'm not too sure if I can continue dating him. What should I do?"

Have sex with him again. The first time usually isn't the best. Folks are nervous and awkward and don't know each other's bodies. If he has the equipment and is willing to learn, he can be taught what works for you. And if he's a bad student or a slow learner, and you just can't deal? Well, then, you can't. And that's fine. Women should feel as entitled to good sex as men do.

Also, STOP FAKING IT. He thinks you liked whatever he did "wrong" and he will keep doing it. You're not obligated to pretend you like it and suffer thru bad sex for his ego.

"I'm used to guys being eager to perform oral sex, but my new partner? Not so much. I haven't brought it up because I have never had to and don't know what to say. I know how guys get when you talk "negative" about their performance, but I have needs as well. How do I approach the subject?"

Men feel entirely entitled to have their needs met. You should feel the same way. Ask him point-blank, "do you eat pussy or nah?" And let him explain. What you want to get from a conversation is whether he's willing to do it and what it takes for him to go down.

I've heard from guys who, in general, have no problem performing oral sex, but will refrain when the woman has an unpleasant odor or isn't well groomed.

"My guy says he likes me and loves the sex, but he wants me to be more sexually aggressive. I've never been the aggressive type. Would like to try, but often times feel awkward. Any suggestions?"

He wants you to initiate sex sometimes so he feels desired as well. This is simple. Rub his penis 3 times: first is an accident, second is a coincidence and third is you clearly initiating sex. Or just give him oral sex. You can never deviate from one of these options and he'll never complain again.

"Husband says frequency of sex matters more than quality so he's not into kissing and foreplay every time. However, I can only have an orgasm with these things. Help!"

Sometimes you just want to skip all the niceties. But if you can only get fully turned on by foreplay, then he needs to do what it takes to get you excited for sex, if for no other reason than it's a better experience for *both* of you. It's unacceptable for him to expect an orgasm, but not put in the effort to work with you to achieve the same.

If you're like most women, when you're turned on, you're more willing to do the "nasty" and "freaky" things that make the sexual experience better for both of you. Explain that to your husband so he understands what he's missing out on by rushing the experience. He should be on board once he realizes what's in it for him.

"My boyfriend ejaculated *on* me. He claims it was a mistake. I don't believe him. I feel he was disrespectful on purpose. I am upset now and feel like shutting him out! How do I approach the situation?"

Ejaculating on your partner is one of those things like hairless vaginas that made its way into real-life sexual interactions because porn normalized it. Everyone doesn't think it's disrespectful and some people actually like it. That said, whether or not he could release on you is a conversation that you two should have had before he did it so he knew where you stood on the issue and to avoid reactions like this.

It likely wasn't a mistake. He meant to do it because he thinks it's sexy. He just didn't expect you to freak out about it— everyone wouldn't— so he's saying it was an accident. Tell him you don't like it and not to do it again.

While you're concerned about disrespect, I am concerned about where the condom was. Why wasn't he wearing one? Did he take it off?

"Some therapists suggest scheduling sex, to which my husband says 'absolutely not!' However, we are both too busy and tired to have

sex. We are happy and healthy, but sex happens 1-2x a month max. Other than scheduling sex, any suggestions to make it happen?"

Since he's not down for scheduling and you both want more sex, what suggestions does he have for ways you two can have more sex? Ask him. You're trying to have sex with him, so you need his input here.

Also, you're not supposed to schedule a sex night. More like a "date night" where you can spend time together and chill and where work/other duties are off-limits. The idea is that the emotional intimacy and relaxed atmosphere will lead to sexual intimacy.

"My fiancé doesn't seem as into sex so I asked what's up. After some pressure he finally gives a list of things I need to improve on such as no body hair ever, no scarf to bed when we have sex and showers before sex. How does one know when to draw the line of wanting to please her man versus being herself?"

You asked what he wanted. He answered. Are you willing to do these things or not? But I need to be honest here, despite him being your fiancé, it doesn't sound like he's attracted to you. All those things he listed are preferences. It's one thing to like them, it's another to totally shut down when he's not getting them.

So you know, the vast majority of men prefer no scarf, cleaned up body hair (not necessarily none) and a fresh shower (though there is a significant population who likes "touched pork", i.e., a shower a few hours ago so your natural scent is present). But when those items aren't present, they're still more than willing to have sex.

"My boyfriend has never been a ravenous, always needing sex kind of guy. I asked him why he doesn't initiate more, he says he will, but it will help if we work out together. I said that means you're not attracted to me. He said, 'yes, I am, but it will help if you get in better shape.' My feelings were hurt. Thoughts?"

So you've probably gained some weight. And I have to give him credit here that he handled the conversation pretty well in that he suggested you work out "together." He's not sitting back complaining. He's willing to put some sweat in the game to achieve the desired result. And he added that he's still attracted to you. As far as weight talks go, your guy did it by the book.

You had an issue you wanted resolved, he gave his suggestion for how the two of you can work together to get the results. No one likes criticism, but you asked him a question and he answered in a non-a--hole way.

It sounds like you have a good guy who wants to get in shape *with you*. Put your feelings aside and tackle getting into better shape *together*. Look at as a way to spend more time together doing something productive, and to get more sex. "Just" working out, whether you lose weight or not, will appeal to him and get you more sex.

"Me and BF got together 3 years ago. He was Mr. Tall & Sexy. I was pretty, but chubby. Fast forward: he's gained the 50 pounds I lost. It's unattractive! I'm put off by his choices as I live a healthy lifestyle— alone. How do I get him to lose weight without being shallow?"

Attraction matters. It's not everything, but it is a thing. And it's devastating to hear that your mate isn't attracted to you or that attraction is dwindling. And yes, that applies to men. Many men care about their looks the same way women do. So you need to tread lightly here.

You're concerned about his looks, but when you're talking to him, all you mention is *health and lifestyle* so you avoid the reaction from the previous query. The next time you're out with him and spot a sexy and fit older couple, point them out and tell him that's your vision for the two of you. Explain that you want to get both of you on track and get *healthier* together. (It does not matter that you are already healthy. This is a "we" issue.)

Start introducing more activity into the relationship, such as suggesting a walk after dinner or a date where you head to the park. Also, invite him to the gym— or wherever you work out— with you. Baby-step your way into making staying active a part of the relationship.

CHAPTER ELEVEN

Dough Matters

There's only one more topic that couples argue about more than sex: money. The tricky thing here is that arguments about money are rarely about money. Money is correlated with control, as well as lifestyle, opportunity, and freedom. So when you're arguing about money with your partner, you're also fussing about that and so much more.

The more mindful you are of that, the easier your discussions about money are. But even when you're trying to negotiate, there are some fundamentals you should be aware of.

"When is it appropriate to ask about finances when you're in a relationship?"

When you're seriously discussing building a life together, when you're moving in together. Do not wait until you are husband and wife (or, wife and wife). The vast majority of people you date won't become a boyfriend, and every boyfriend doesn't become husband. Everyone you're in like, or even love with doesn't need your financial details.

The exception here is when your partner asks you to borrow money. You want to be paid back, so knowledge of his or her finances is a completely acceptable request, as is a signed agreement to make sure you get paid back in a timely fashion. You don't give money without knowing how you will get it back... with interest.

"How much detail should engaged couples get into about finances? I have no debt of my own and it sounds selfish, but I'm not ready to take on anyone else's debt. Should this have been discussed pre-engagement?"

It's fine to discuss as an engaged couple. But if you're not willing to face the potential of taking on someone else's debt, you probably shouldn't be considering marriage. As a wife, you become responsible for the debts your partner accumulates.

If your partner has pre-existing debt that you're not willing to take on, you should have a conversation about what he plans to do to get his financial affairs in order before the marriage as even if you're not responsible for his debt, his debts affect what he's financially able to contribute to the household.

CREDIT/DEBT

"I have very bad credit that I'm working on repairing. I'm in a relationship with a very nice guy who seemingly has everything together. I'm very embarrassed by this, however, I want to be honest. When is the appropriate time to discuss this issue?"

You can be honest at any point about the debt you're facing. You're only obligated when you're engaged (and married).

Also, just because someone appears to have everything together, doesn't mean they actually do. But if he's one of those rare people, talk to him about your situation, as much to be honest as to see if he can offer any insight as to how to get back in good standing. You should also consider contacting a credit repair service.

"I love my BF, but he is horrible with money and in massive debt. A small part of me thinks I should leave now before our relationship

gets more serious. He says he's "working on it", but he's 33. Are bad spending habits and financial issues enough to be a deal breaker?"

That is definitely enough reason to exit a relationship, or at least not to mingle his finances with your own in a live-in arrangement or at the marriage-level, as his poor decision making will have adverse effect on your finances.

Before bailing, inquire further as to exactly what he is doing to "work on it". If he's putting in actual effort—not just talk— to correct the mistakes of his past, then work with him. Also, age is just a number. There is no definitive time to get your life together— or not. It's a matter of being aware of the issue, and *doing something* to either prevent it or fix it.

"I co-signed for a loan for an ex years ago when I was young and stupid. He recently stopped paying and hasn't returned my calls. Bank is calling me non-stop and I made a payment to avoid impacting my credit report. After Google-ing him, I found out his mother passed last month. Is it insensitive of me to expect him to make arrangements for payment? It's affecting my life and my credit. After all, he hasn't reached out to tell me anything."

Not insensitive at all. It's sad that his mother has passed, but a relative, even an immediate one passing, isn't an excuse to abandon real-world responsibilities, like payments.

Let him know that you're being contacted about the payments that he is primarily responsible for. Hopefully, he's "just" overwhelmed, the payment slipped his mind, and he will handle it expeditiously. If not, you're legally responsible for the payment, and unless you want to ruin your credit, you need to pay up.

HIS MONEY IS FUNNY

"My "man friend" (we've been bedding it for 2 years) asked to borrow money. I don't lend, but I could afford to spare, so I gifted it. He insisted on giving it back. I genuinely consider us friends *with benefits*. Is this inappropriate?"

You're FWB asked for a loan? Huh? You're dealing with a husband headache from your FWB. Just sex. That's it. It's time to find a new, stress-free situation. FWBs aren't supposed to be complicated.

You are not an ATM. But you decided to give him money like you were Bank of America. So yes, he should pay you back. Because that's what the bank requires when it loans money.

I need you to pick up Suze Orzman's book, *Women & Money: Owning the Power to Control Your Destiny*, immediately. Orzman, a financial guru, refers to loaning money to friends and family, and especially without interest, as one of the top 5 money mistakes that women can't afford to make.

On Oprah.com Orzman recommends saying "no" when asked to loan money: "Sometimes the most thoughtful gift is to say no: No, because you're unwilling to enable their poor habits. No, because they need to save themselves. No, because giving what they're asking for could erode your own financial security."

If you do decide to *lend* money in the future, at the very least, have the borrower sign a promissory note and establish a payment plan (with dates) for when your money will be returned. If the borrower can't agree to those terms, then he/she can't access your funds.

"BF is strapped for cash. He has car repairs, school, family stuff and he's trying to help his family financially. How much do I help? I feel helpless."

You don't financially help. That is not your role as a girlfriend. If he needs a listening ear while he talks though his frustrations, you listen. If he wants to brainstorm strategies to make more money or where he can cut back or even who he can borrow money from, you're all in.

You know the coffers are light right now, so don't add to his financial burden by suggesting pricey dates. Stick to inexpensive or free outings, such as museums, parks, art galleries, etc., where you can have fun and be mindful of the budget.

"My hubs loathes his job. He's belittled and disrespected by his boss. I told him to quit and look for something else. Things would be tight for us, but we could manage on my salary. My bestie says I'll be resentful for carrying finances as woman. Am I crazy for making this suggestion?"

You're not crazy. Your *husband* is in a bad spot and you naturally want to see him happy and appreciated. And you have the income to make it happen.

Before you suggest he quit, help him re-work his resume and look for another job. Together, strategize for finding a new employer and set a timetable for when he can quit. Knowing that there's an end date and actively trying to get out of the situation should lift his spirits and give him something to look forward to.

"My man has hit a rough spot financially. We agreed that if one can't help the other then we

would be honest and say "no." What should I do when he gets mad that I won't help him?"

Let him be mad and stand firm in your "no." He is not entitled to your money (and nor are you entitled to his.) You don't have it to give without upsetting your own finances and what you won't do is put yourself in a bad or tight financial spot to help a man who is not your husband.

Help him look for a job, or a better paying job or an additional part-time job so he can cover his bills. But you do not reach into your pocketbook or account to cover his expenses.

"I'm scared for my relationship. My boyfriend was laid-off last year and is now having financial problems, and he seems depressed. It's causing us to argue a lot. I try my best to be supportive and loving, but he just seems like he's giving up on everything. He says it's not me. I want to help, but what to do?"

It's not you; it's him. Being "let go"— whether it's called laid off, downsized or fired— will be a blow to most people's self-esteem. They will feel incompetent and unappreciated, and some will become resentful. Combine those feelings with the stress of being unable to find work, with bills piling up and money running low and things can be disastrous.

When I was dealing with an unemployed man, the conventional advice I heard about how to "manage" was to let him know that you believe in him, assure him of your loyalty to the relationship, encourage his spirits with positive words and help him look for work by revamping his résumé or searching for job leads with him. The unconventional advice suggested that I cheer him up by putting it on him as often as possible and put off his creditors by paying his bills.

Does all that sound like BS? It should. Every woman I've spoken to who has been in a relationship with a man who's been laid off or fired has told me that she tried all of those tips, even the unconventional ones, and it was all in vain. (From personal experience: I did everything but pay bills. And none of that helped.)

"We made it because I put my head down and got through it," one woman told me. In other words, she practiced patience, adopted an uncanny ability to ignore the worst of her partner's newfound traits and just plain hoped that her man would someday be transformed back into the person she fell in love with rather than the frustrated lump he'd become. The good news: when he found a job, he went back to normal.

"I met a guy who is sweet and honest, but can't find a job. He sleeps on friends couches if they let him. What are your thoughts on dating a man who's down on his luck?"

No. The type of man who you actually want to date, wouldn't even consider dating if these were his circumstances. He's not able to provide the basics for himself, like shelter. His sole focus needs to be on finding a job and stable living conditions. I'm sure your guy is as awesome as you say, but he isn't fit to date right now, not you or anyone else.

TRICKING/ GIFTS

"How do you feel about buying things for your man (other than birthdays and holidays)?"

Small gifts that fit comfortably into your budget are fine, especially when he does the same for you. That said, I'm not a fan of splurging unless you're married. Most boyfriend-girlfriend relationships are temporary and making big ticket financial investments on relationships that don't last isn't fiscally responsible.

"Boyfriend said not to do anything for him or give him money if I'm going to complain about the way he treats me. I don't give to receive, but my point is he doesn't seem to put much thought towards me. How do I explain this to him without sounding like I'm bitching again?"

You have no business giving him money. He's not your husband or your son. You're a girlfriend participating in a "wife duty".

Also, not that you're doing things for him in order to get him to act right, but if he's not treating you the way you want to be treated, stop buying him stuff. You don't reward bad behavior and go gifting for a guy that "doesn't seem to put much thought" towards you.

Skip the "I do XYZ for you, so you should do ABC for me," conversation, and just tell him what you want from him. If he can't put some effort into being considerate, then you need a new boyfriend.

"A FWB came to visit me last week. I paid for his train ticket. It's the third time I've done this. We go to the movies and he doesn't pay. But when I say something, he snaps and refuses to speak to me the whole weekend. Help!"

Is his name Tyrone? It sounds like you're *allowing yourself* to be used. If he can't afford to come see you, then he doesn't need to come, period. He's an FWB. His job description is to blow your back out and not give you headaches.

Sex with no commitment is easy to come by in every city, town, or state. There is absolutely no reason to have to pay for access to it. Surely, you can find a man that you don't have to import to your city and who doesn't get fussy like a child when he's called out on sucking you financially dry.

"Is it ever ok to accept money from a BF? I didn't ask for it, he offered after I mentioned wanting to take a 6-week course for work. My gut reaction was to thank him for the offer and decline. I felt some kinda way taking money from him. Bestie says I'm bugging and should've accepted his help."

Go with your gut. You're not an ATM, neither is he. And while it's a nice gesture, he is not responsible for that expense.

"The 'your BF/GF is not an ATM' doesn't really fly. If a woman is giving up 'the box' to a man, there for him when he needs her, cooking if she wants, supports him, etc., then what is wrong with him giving her money? I'm in a relationship doing all this, but when my car breaks down I still gotta call my Dad?"

Call Dad— or another relative. Or your bank and transfer money from your savings. If you have a car, you, as a responsible adult, should have money set aside to fix it when it breaks down.

Also, for everything you just listed, you've already received an equivalent from him. When you "gave up the box", you also got some good D, no? He's also there for you emotionally when you need him too, no? (And if not, why are you together?) He cooks too, no? And if not, he's supplied food in the form of date-night dinners, right? He's already "paid" you back for what you do for him by doing the *exact same* thing for you. Money for your car isn't an even exchange.

Are you comfy with your man running to you for money? If no, then why should you be running to him for it?

"That makes no sense. As a grown woman your father isn't responsible for you. Any parental financial help is nice, not duty. Men are not ATMs, but gifts can be harmless."

Your Dad is responsible for you if you are single. Any decent father would agree. But your man is definitely *not* responsible. If you have to ask someone for money and you are single, your dad is in line before your man. If your man wants to be the go-to that you depend on, he needs to be your husband.

Gifts are not harmless. They cost money. And it's foolish for a man to splurge on expensive gifts for a woman who is not his wife. It's a bad investment, especially if you are not returning the favor.

"In all the relationships you've had, a man has never purchased a bracelet, necklace, expensive perfume, or paid a bill? That's ridiculous. You gave away a lot of free pussy then."

Ma'am! I am not prostitute. I do not have sex in exchange for money or gifts. If access to your lady parts is the price of a bracelet, necklace, perfume bottle or a bill, you're selling it for cheap. Raise your prices!

Have sex because you want to have it. If you're doing it in exchange for gifts, don't do for depreciating assets, including jewelry as even the re-sell value on diamonds is low. Make him buy gifts that *appreciate* after they are purchased—homes, art, stock, etc. Or take straight cash and invest it in the market, or into a business. Don't leave a relationship with a big spender with nothing but expensive accessories, stale perfume, and memories of a lifestyle you can't sustain on your own.

"Why is it not OK to ever accept financial help from BF? When me and hubs dated, we exchanged $20 here or there. I don't see how a woman can expect or be comfortable with a man to pay for dates but not be ok with him loaning a few bucks back and forth. Couldn't one say just go Dutch because 'I'm not an ATM"?'"

A twenty exchanged here and there when you're short is one thing. You're talking about a relatively insignificant sum of money and you break even in the end because the money flows both ways.

Paying bills, buying expensive gifts, and paying GFs school bills is an *entirely* different situation from what you're asking about. The most jarring difference is it's a much larger sum of money and it's not being reimbursed down the line.

Also, a date isn't an exchange of money between partners, it's a bill paid to a third-party to cover the cost of a shared experience that you both benefit from. I also advocate that women participate in the dating process by paying for every 3 to 4 dates.

"Boyfriend paid for my half of a vacation because I couldn't afford to go with him. After getting other opinions, he feels I should pay him back when I am able to and says that I shouldn't have allowed him to pay for the whole thing in the first place. He is the one that offered. Do I owe him anything?"

I'm going to guess that you two didn't have the type of or frequency of sex he expected on the trip, and he didn't feel he got the return he wanted on his investment. Am I right?

This is an obvious example that backs up my assertion about why you shouldn't accept large gifts from boyfriends. He offered, you accepted, and now he's claiming you owe him for what he spent *after the fact.* This is shady and very distasteful.

You don't owe him anything. But if you want to stay in this relationship— and I wouldn't really suggest it given his level of grimy, but that's your call— you have to pay him or give him what he wants to shut him up.

This is a horrible position to be in, one he set up intentionally, and exactly why I tell women not to accept big ticket items from boyfriends. More often than not, they want something in return and will not hesitate to ask for it.

"My ex paid for me to go to school while we were together. During an argument after our breakup he said he wishes he never did it and I probably won't finish anyway. I want to give him his money back but it'll literally be all of my savings. I don't want to be broke or a charity case. What should I do?"

I would have told you upfront not to take the money, just because I hear a lot of stories like this one, where a guy gives his girlfriend money, then holds it over her head when she doesn't do what he wants. But the money is spent now. And you don't owe him anything for the generosity he provided during the relationship.

That sting you've felt since he said that? That's ego. Don't screw your finances to quiet it. If later in life, you want to pay him back, do so. Or you could just sent him a copy of your degree with a "Thank you" note attached.

After I posted my answer to her query, she responded again with advice for the readers : "If something seems too good to be true (like a guy giving you tens of thousands of dollars and wanting nothing in return), it usually is! I had to pay back him back with my pride, a belittling and degrading feeling, but a great lesson nonetheless. Never again!"

"Am I crazy for turning down a sponsor? He actually enjoys wining and dining me and blowing money on shopping sprees for me. But I know that he does the same for other women as well."

You're not crazy; you're smart. No man, except maybe your father is splurging on you just to see a smile on your face. Your sponsor doesn't enjoy wining and dining as much as he does the deference and sexual benefits he gets from it. It's an investment in his happiness (or ego).

He spends and you want him to keep it up. So when he's late, or doesn't answer the phone or has other women, you remain silent. And when you want something, you butter him up to get it. And when he buys something really over the top, he expects to be "thanked" in accordance with his splurge. It's not free. You're expected to pay him back, on your back. Or knees.

MARRIED PEOPLE
(THE RULES ARE DIFFERENT)

"How do I bring up an issue with bills to my husband? Everything else is great in the relationship and I hate disturbing the peace, but I've asked him 3 times to take care of something and he has not. I know that he should have the money, why hasn't he done it?"

Everything isn't great. Your husband isn't handling the basics and the relationship is only peaceful because you're not speaking up about what you're concerned about. You have to say something before your annoyance leads to full-blown resentment. Ask him point-blank why he's not taking care of what you've asked of him. And too, ask if he has the money. Either he doesn't have it, or he's avoiding the payment in some passive aggressive manner because he's upset with you about something.

"I recently added my new husband to my credit card, which I explained is for trips and emergencies. I see he's used the credit card for lunches, haircuts and shoes. Should I take the card back? Credit is very important to me."

Taking the card back without having a conversation with him is going to start a war. If he gave you something and took it back without a conversation, you would be pissed. He's your husband, another adult. Don't "son" him like he's a child.

Reiterate to your husband what the card is for and the importance of great credit. You may have to lay out clearly what counts as an emergency and what isn't

If he can't get it right after a talk, tell him that you think it best to have separate cards and you will remove his name from yours.

"My husband is terrible with finances. He's late depositing checks, and overspends. I now handle the money, but we still have problems with his spending. I don't want to force him to cut up his credit card but I'm not sure what to do. He's great, except with money and I'm a stickler when it comes to cash/ bills?"

You can't force him to cut up his card. He's your husband, not your child. Asking him not to use a credit card is a last resort measure.

A lot of people weren't taught about money—how to spend it, how to save it, how to invest it, *nothing*. Or even the purpose of it, which is to make more money. And many people acquired bad financial habits from their parents.

Tell your husband you're concerned about the finances and suggest taking a money management class together. It may also help if you establish financial goals as a couple and give him something to work toward other than just paying bills. He may not see the pay off in being responsible.

"Wait! Why should she have to take a money class together when that's not her issue. If she was bad at head would you suggest that they take a class on head together?"

It's a "we" issue. As a married couple, they are in this financial situation together. If his money is funny, so is hers. And yes, if she was bad at oral sex, I would suggest they take a class on it— yes, they exist— because they are having sex *together*. His penis is involved, he should know what she's learning to do with it. Just like she should know what he's learning about his finances since they affect the household that she also contributes to.

"I found out my husband has four checking accounts that my name is not on. He also will not add my name. We share a joint account but there is rarely enough money to cover bills. I don't want to give ultimatums but the multiple accounts make me think he doesn't see forever with me. I've said this to him, but no change. What now?"

There are multiple issues here. Your husband is keeping big secrets from you, not carrying his financial weight in the relationship and instead he's choosing to cover his other bases and not home. And he's not communicating when you ask what's going on. What he's up to could be the level of a mistress, a secret child, or like you imply, he's planning an exit.

As a rule, I'm not a fan of ultimatums. People tend to whip them out too soon and often don't follow through on the promise. But given the level of secrecy and lack of communication, there's a worthy exception to be made here. Tell him, "if you don't come clean, I will [insert whatever you are prepared to do]." You get one shot here. If you don't follow through with your promise, your credibility is forever damaged and things will get worse.

CHAPTER TWELVE

Family Bidness

My parents have one rule about dealing with each other's families: "you handle your family." They like the other spouse's people just fine, and they hang out with them, visit with them and everything goes well. But when there's conflict between a spouse and their people? The blood-related spouse leads on how to proceed and the other spouse supports that position.

Here's the thing: by the time you show up in someone's life, they've dealt with their family for at least two decades and some change. There are rivalries, backstories, allegiances and drama that you aren't privy to and those dynamics all come into play when folks get to squabbling.

Your role is to stay out of it, support your partner (at the very least in public) and keep your mouth shut to his (or her) people, even when you're married-in. (You're family, but not blood.) This advice goes double for girlfriends and mother-of-child scenarios. You quickly will get your card pulled about the lacking status of your relationship if you don't follow it.

"I've had it with my boyfriend's mother. We've been together for two years, and she calls him constantly to ask him to run an errand for her, fix something for her at the house or take her somewhere. Whenever we have a disagreement, I can count on him telling his mother about what's going on between us, and she always sides against me. When I complain, he tells me I'm overreacting. She's also made it clear that she doesn't like me and has said in front of me that she preferred my boyfriend's ex-girlfriend, who remains in contact with her. The last straw was when she invited his ex to a family cookout that she knew I would attend. I left, but my boyfriend didn't. He said he didn't want to insult his mother. Before that incident, we were discussing moving in together. Am I wrong for not agreeing to move in until this situation is resolved?"

There's nothing wrong with a man having a close relationship with his mother or even having her as a priority in his life. I wouldn't trust (without some extreme back-story) a man who wasn't given to *occasionally* running an errand for his mom, fixing or installing something in her home or spending time with her. But your guy is taking things way too far.

Your main problem isn't your boyfriend's mother though; *it's your boyfriend.* It may be easier for you to blame her for the problems in your relationship so you can avoid confronting him about his behavior. Mom couldn't side with him about an argument if he wasn't telling her about the relationship. And she probably would like you if he weren't telling her about your fights. Even if she did like the ex better, she'd show more respect if her son demanded she did. He doesn't.

Despite the lack of boundaries— yours with him and his with his mother — you have chosen to stay for two years. This has sent the message that their behavior is OK. Stop complaining and lay out what boundaries you need him to create with his mother if he wants to continue a relationship with you.

Finally, the conversation about whether you should move in should be tabled until you see positive change *over a period of time.*

"My BF's ex GF is still close with his mother. She even calls her "mom", they have been broken up for over a year and they no longer communicate. Am I wrong for wanting this relationship to stop? It is awkward at family functions when both of us are around."

It's ridiculous to ask you to come to his family events with his ex there. And it's ridiculous for him to go, too, and play into his mother's manipulative games. Tell your boyfriend that you're tired of being made to feel awkward, and that he has to force his mother's hand by not showing up to family events where the ex is present. He has to give a clear ultimatum to his mother that it's either his ex or him.

His mom likes his ex. A lot. But she's not going to place her relationship with him in jeopardy over her relationship with his ex.

Hopefully, by finally putting your foot down, you'll get his attention. If he's not willing to change? Well, then, it's time to change boyfriends. He will be okay. He has his ex and his mother to keep him warm at night.

"My boyfriend is upset because I left his family's party without him knowing. The feud between his mother and me came to a head at the event. She told me I wasn't good enough for her son because I'm African-American, I don't have an Ivy League degree, I have kinky hair, I don't come from wealth, etc. I told him I was done, but he's upset because I won't hear his side. Do I owe him that?"

Anyone would be upset after being told she isn't good enough for any reason. You have a right to be offended, and if your date said this to you, I would applaud you leaving and encourage you to get out of that relationship. That would be an occasion where storming out is entirely acceptable. But the scenario you described is not that. His mother was out of line, but she is not him; nor is she his representative. You took it out on him even though *he isn't the problem.*

You owe him a conversation. Being walked out on isn't only embarrassing, especially in a room full of relatives, it also indicates a lack of respect. You should have asked your man to take you home or, at least, walk you to the car. If he'd refused, it would have been fine to go. If you want to break off the relationship because of his mother, you're entitled to, but you need to tell him that.

On the off chance that you want to salvage this relationship— and it can be salvaged, since he wants to be "heard out"— apologize to him for walking out and ignoring his attempts to contact you. Add that he has to talk to his mother about respecting you. She doesn't have to like you, but she also can't insult you. Let him know you're not attending a family event anytime soon. He probably won't ask you anyway.

Six months later, she was back with an update... and a new story.

"I contacted you months ago about me leaving my man's family's party without his knowledge after his mom yelled at me. You were right. I was in the wrong, then and now. I recently got into a shouting match with his mother. My boyfriend brushed her behavior off and we aren't talking because of it. He says I disrespected her by yelling. Was I wrong? My mom I said I shouldn't argue with any Mama besides my own. Seriously? He's amazing I don't want her to be our downfall. How do I make her like me and see I'm worthy of him?"

Listen to your Mom. You don't argue with your man's mama, much less yell. What were you thinking?

When Mom got to talking reckless, your move was to turn to your man and say you want to leave. *Now.* And in the car, you tell him he must speak to his mother. She doesn't have to like you, but being disrespectful is not acceptable. And you don't go back around her until he says he has handled it.

Between you yelling at his mom, and you walking out on him, I'm amazed you two are still together. I'm shocked that he asked you to another family event and you agreed to go— and that you couldn't hold your temper long enough not to blow it. Again. I would suggest, again, that you avoid his family events.

His Mom isn't going to like you. She doesn't like African-Americans, which you can't do anything about, and your behavior around her has confirmed every stereotype she has of American-born Blacks. An apology for raising your voice may help. But honestly? You should avoid her unless this relationship progresses to an engagement.

"I've been dating this guy for five months now. He is very nice, but I have never met his parents. It seems that there is always an excuse why we can't see them. I guess I'm being paranoid, but I'm not sure he wants his folks to meet me, since I'm a Black lady and he's white. I keep telling myself it's 2013, but ... "

Women often take not meeting his family as a sign that a guy isn't (getting) serious about them, but it's a misguided worry. Several years ago, in my former life as the relationships editor at *Essence*, I used to conduct roundtable discussions with men about dating and relationships. One of them was about meeting the parents. I thought I was lobbing a softball question to get the conversation rolling: "Of course it means something ... right?" I asked the guys.

The guys stared at me blankly. One finally took pity on me after an awkward silence and asked, "Is it supposed to mean something? Do women think it means something?" If so, he, and many other guys, had missed the memo. Another said there was sort of an unspoken agreement that he could bring home as many women as he liked, and everyone would play along as if each woman was special. In case you're wondering if this is cultural, two of the men were African, two American, and one from the Caribbean.

I'm sure to some men, it's a big deal to take a woman home, but for others it's as simple as not wanting to be alone— yes, guys get lonely, too— and wanting someone to spend time with. I've read *plenty* of stories from women who tell of bonding with a guy's mom and siblings, and vacationing with his family, only to find out that he had another long-term girlfriend and the family spent time with her, too. (No one ever says anything because it's *his family*, not yours.)

If you want to know how he feels about you, ask and then watch his actions (they should align). And if you're still really concerned about why you haven't met his parents, ask about that, too, instead of jumping to one of the worst-possible conclusions.

It's possible that his parents could have a problem with you being Black, but let's avoid assuming that all members of the older white set are raging racists. Unless your boyfriend has given you some indication that his parents would have a problem with your race, then you may be jumping to conclusions.

YOUR KIDS

The smallest members of the family can come with some pretty big hurdles. Dating and building relationships are tough enough as a child-free woman, but the kiddos rev up the intensity. It's no longer about what works for you, but your child(ren), possibly his, managing your ex, and your potential new boo, too.

Find out how what's going on in the lives of these single moms (and dads):

"I have 15-year-old twin girls and they don't meet a guy until I'm in a relationship. You've said wait a couple of seasons while dating to be sure you're not dating his representative. When is the right time to introduce him to my daughters?"

There's a popular relationship expert who suggests that a new man should meet your children upfront. It's irresponsible and unfathomable, given the frequent horror stories about boyfriends who abuse their mate's children. I'm not saying every man will do that, but every man should be properly vetted by you to assure it's not a possibility. The same way you date a man for seasons to see his ups and downs and if his words consistently line up with his actions to make sure he's right for you? That's doubly important when you're bringing him around the kids.

You've got it right. Your primary role as a parent is to protect your children. That means you don't just bring anybody to meet your kids. I don't want any man you're dating to meet your children if he hasn't been around for at least 4-6 months and he should be *at least* talking about a relationship, if not offering one.

"Belle, my son is going through the 'Terrible Twos' times 10. He can be, for lack of better words, a terror— crying, meltdowns over everything, and screaming. Anyway, I'm dating a guy for a few months now and want to introduce him to my son but I'm afraid this might scare him off. What should I do?"

If he has kids, fine. If not, wait. Parents know that a child acting up at that age is completely normal, but that will scare off someone without kids. Also, if it's not heading toward a committed relationship, he shouldn't be around your son. Meeting your kid is a privilege.

"I've had 3 serious relationships that produced three kids. My current boyfriend said he wants a child with me too. He is a good person and will be a good father. The problem is, I don't know if I want more children. Should I just give him what he wants and learn to love the child?"

Hell no! Children are not gifts you give a man like it's Christmas Day. That is not a way for you to prove you really love someone who may be jealous that you've made a child for three other people, but not him. The primary responsibility of raising a child falls on the mom. You know this because you have three children already. If you're not up for having more babies, or unsure, don't do it. *Period.*

Also, it would be irresponsible of me not to point out a pattern here. You have three children by three men who have not committed to you. What will make this fourth man any different? Kids don't make men stay. You know this from personal experience three times over. If you want this man to be committed to you, and hopefully you do if you're contemplating having a child for him, tell him you want a ring and a signed marriage license to even consider another child.

"Bad blood between my baby daddy and me. He started dating someone when I was 7 months pregnant. Never helped me prep for the baby and doesn't do much to help now. We're not on speaking terms. I'm still allowed to be mad, right?"

You don't need permission to be angry. But I have to ask, what is it doing for you? You being mad doesn't make him show up for the child you created together. It doesn't do anything but stifle you.

He hasn't said "I'm sorry" or asked for your forgiveness, but forgive him anyway, *for you.* You're walking around mad at the world for dealing you this hand, mad at yourself for falling for him, mad that your baby doesn't have a dad who shows up, and mad that he's not there for you, doesn't change your circumstance.

Forgive him so you will feel better. And when you feel better, pick up the phone and ask him to come see about his child. Not because you're not doing an A+ job on your own, but because your baby deserves to know who his dad is and have him be a part of his life. And what's best for the baby trumps whatever bad blood there is between the parents.

"My 6-year-old told her father that my boyfriend stayed over the last two nights. I told her not to talk about what goes on in my house with her father, especially since my boyfriend and her dad don't get along, to the point that they don't speak. I also discovered that her father has been bribing her to get information about me and my boyfriend. What do I do?"

Your daughter isn't the problem here. She's 6, and she's doing what children her age do: observe and talk about it. A young child should not be responsible for guarding her mother's secrets.

No matter how you may feel about your ex, he's an active participant in your child's life, and you should encourage your daughter to have an open and honest relationship with him. By asking her to keep secrets from her father, you are implying that he is somehow outside of the family circle of trust. She may not live in the home with him or see him on a day-to-day basis, but she should be comfortable speaking with him about whatever she wants, including your business. It's selfish to erode the relationship between them to serve your own interests.

Your ex is also wrong. He should know better than to use his daughter as a pawn to get intel on you and your boyfriend. Even if it doesn't take much to get good information from most 6-year-olds, bribing her is manipulative.

The quick fix here is to make sure your daughter has no grown business to tell your ex. Keep your daughter in the dark about the juicy details of what you're up to. Have your guy spend the night when your daughter is visiting her father or other times when she is out of the house.

"My children's father is very hands-on: picks them up from school every day, feeds them dinner, then brings them to me. It works because I get off late. My problem is my boy-friend/ soon-to-be ex. He doesn't like that their father is hands on. My question is, is this something that I'll have to deal with dating as a single mom?"

He's dysfunctional. There's no drama between you and the children's father and the man takes care of his children. Most men would see that as a blessing. Your soon-to-be ex gotta go. Quick.

I'm going to guess your boyfriend wasn't raised with his dad, and he is threatened by the amount of time the father puts in because you seeing what a good man looks like in action gives you high expectations, likely ones that your boyfriend can't live up to.

"The woman that my daughter's father is da-ting told him he does too much for us! This came out of his mouth by accident. I don't want this girl around my child anymore. He doesn't do anything out if the ordinary. Just the basics, which is good with me. She's caus-ing unnecessary stress. Overreacting?"

She feels like she can't compete and she's mad he has other priorities. She doesn't feel he does for her what he does for you and the kid.

Have a conversation about your concerns before you make demands. Talk to him, about what she said and how she treats the child. If he's doing great things as a dad and a co-parent, he is also invested in what's best for the kid.

She followed up with an update...

"I spoke to him, which ended in a argument. No one should come in and disrupt what's been good for four years. He's pissed because I told him to deal with her before bringing her around the baby again. This girl is a pain in the behind. I don't do messy. She's the queen of messy."

Um. This wasn't the solution we discussed. That chat would have gone over better if you expressed your concern and *asked* him to address her about the comments. Do you like being told what to do? Would you be okay with your ex telling you how to run your new relationship?

The woman may be a pain, she may also be delusional. But she's there. And when he argues with you, all he does is tell her and she tells him, "see? Unappreciative. I told you." It's not true, of course, but he's pissed at you and more easily influenced by her perspective then.

You gotta find a way to deal with this without driving a wedge between you and ex who has been a great co-parent thus far. Circle back quickly, apologize for your role in the argument, and express concern *for the child*. Both of you want what is best for kid. *Ask him what he thinks* is the best course of action here. When people *feel included* in solutions, they respond better.

"Belle, I've been divorced for 2 yrs. My ex and I have a son. I'd like to start dating again, but every time a new guy meets my ex, they lose interest. My ex is a big guy, and he's told guys that he would kill them if they ever touched my son. It's been a couple of months, and I feel helpless. Help me!"

Your ex is an a— and he's doing this to control you, not out of concern for the child. You have to check him, and stop introducing people to him. Your ex-husband doesn't have to approve your dates, and the new guys shouldn't be around your kid anyway, so there should be no risk to the child. You may need to get a guy around your ex's size (or bigger) so he can stop that silly ish.

"I am married to a wonderful man, and we have a child together. He loves my oldest son like his own and has been in my son's life since he was 2. After four years, my ex now decides that he wants to see my child and wants me to let my son come over to him. My son never asks about him, ever. He feels like my husband is his father. I know my husband's reaction will be, "f— him. He wasn't around. Why is he calling now?" I feel like I would be wrong if I tell the ex, "No, you can't see my child, beat it. Don't you have, like, three other kids somewhere?" He is a deadbeat. I'm so confused and scared to tell my husband. I don't want him to feel disrespected. What should I do?"

For whatever reason, your ex has decided that it's time to do what he should have been doing all along. If he wants to have a relationship with his child, put aside the discomfort you may have and focus on at least letting the child's father try to forge a bond with his son. Tell your husband before you do anything, and ask what he thinks. Have a conversation.

If you do not include your husband in the decision for your ex and your son to meet, you are going to put your marriage in hell. Tell your husband about your ex's request and let him be mad at the unmitigated gall of your son's father. Do not make him feel you've betrayed or disrespected him by not consulting him on an issue that affects the child he has been raising.

It probably seems a little unfair that your ex can show up out of the blue uninvited like some sort of Adele lyric and expect to be taken seriously. Still, for all that he hasn't done (or paid), he's still the child's father, and that carries a lot of weight, at least enough for a *supervised* visit. At this point, I do not suggest you leave your child with a person he barely knows and you barely talk to, even if he's the biological father.

HIS KIDS

"In a relationship with a divorced man. We both want the same things as far as getting married and having children. However, I don't like the fact that we won't be experiencing marriage and having children for the first time together since he's already done these things. Should I just get over it?"

You don't like one of the fundamental traits that come with dating a divorced man with children. If you want to be with him, then you have to get over it. That's the only solution here. There is no DeLorean to hop in next to Michael J. Fox and go back in time to change the past.

"BF and I are discussing marriage. He has 10-year-old son. He's the first guy I've dated with a kid and I'm struggling with the child support aspect knowing that his child's mom will technically "eat before we do". She also gets upset when we take trips or make expensive purchases and threatens to increase child support. What do I do?"

The *child eats* before you. Unless your man's a wealthy CEO, athlete or rapper, the child support isn't enough to trick on the mom and kid. And the kid *should be* his priority. You don't want a man who doesn't put his own blood first. If you can't deal, now is the time to go your separate ways as that won't change until the child is grown.

He needs to get a handle on the situation with the child's mother. She's got some resentment, hence the threats. And no matter how much he gives, it will never be enough if she feels she should be in your shoes.

See it from her POV, which I know is hard. She has a child by him, she likely didn't see herself as a single mom, and then he decides to build a life with a woman that doesn't have kids or even his kid. And he does things with you that he may not have done for her or that he used to do with her. That hurts.

"I'm talking to a guy that really wants to be with me. I like him a lot. Only problem is he has a daughter. I don't have children and went through crazy baby mama drama with my ex who had a child. Now I don't want to date a man with kids. Should I not go out with him because of this?"

He's not the guy before him. And is there anything to indicate that his ex is anything like the previous guy's ex? Every man doesn't come with "baby mama drama". Some folks are actually, like, adults, and co-parent without being combative. You rarely hear of them, because they're not causing any drama worth talking about in a status update.

That said, if you don't want to date him, then don't. You're not obligated to. But I wouldn't block him because of how your ex's ex behaved.

"Dating a guy with a child (3 years). Out of my comfort zone, but not a deal breaker. Great guy, however, he's been out of a relationship with the child's mom less than a year (9 mos). That's what really concerns me. What is the best way to bring it up without sounding insecure?"

It's a valid question. Also, it's okay to be emotionally vulnerable. You like him and you want to know if he's worth getting serious about. So just ask, "I like you, but I'm also concerned about the length of time it's been since your last relationship. Do you think you'll get back with your child's mother?" Also ask why they broke up. Was it a big fight and an abrupt ending? There's a greater possibility they'll get back together if it was a big blow up than if there were a plethora of problems and the relationship eroded over time.

"I'm feeling some type of way... BF's kid is in the hospital in another state. BF is going to see his kid. I asked him where he was staying

overnight, he said mother of child's home. Mother of child has a BF so I shouldn't trip, right?"

Uh.... It's not appropriate to stay at another non-relative woman's house, even if she is the mother of child. They have hotel rooms wherever he's headed and I'm pretty sure her man doesn't know of this arrangement.

Here's the catch-22 though, you look ass-y for bringing this up *right now*. The only issue you're supposed to be concerned about is the sick child.

You know I'm not a fan of dropping big money on boyfriends, but this is an emergency. Offer to get him a hotel room, "so you'll be more comfortable, Bae", or you go with him, and you either b*oth* stay at the ex's or you both stay in a hotel.

"I'm 28, well-educated and a relatively nice woman. I recently met a guy who meets every item on my list... but he has three young children, each of whom has a different mother. How many children/BMs are too many?"

Nope. And that answer isn't because you're educated or even nice. I would say that to any woman who is not in a similar position as him. He's shown a three-peat pattern of impregnating women and not committing to them. Unless you're down to be the fourth mother of his child, he is not a suitable option.

It's just too many people to deal with, and if he's doing fatherhood like he's supposed to (and not just being an Instagram dad), he's spreading himself too thin for a relationship.

"What is your opinion on staying in a marriage for the sake of the kids? (Granted there isn't any abuse or anything?)"

It's noble, but it's setting a bad precedent of what relationships are supposed to be. And if you and hubs are both miserable, the kids start wondering why you're together at the latest around the age of 10. (The little ones are way more perceptive than we give them credit for.) And because the first primary relationship they saw was unfulfilling, they may grow up to think they have to stay in unhealthy relationships because that's what you're "supposed" to do.

Instead of accepting misery, you and hubs should consider heading to a therapist or counselor to see if you can find some happy in your marriage. Marriages can go through low periods and that's entirely normal. But you can get back to a great place if *you and your spouse* are willing to work. As *Divorce Court's* Judge Lynn Toler told me when I interviewed her for my "Ask Demetria" column on TheRoot.com: "At almost any stage in a marriage, you can get back to where you need to be. You can get back to where it's acceptable, and once you're at acceptable you can get to better;

from better you can get to good. There's hope as long as *both parties* are still engaged."

CHAPTER THIRTEEN

Friends or Frenemies?

They are the "family" that you get to choose. And while they may not be "blood", they can come with complications like they are. Just like with actual family members, you can't just dismiss them when they tick you off. I mean, you can, but you don't *want to*, especially when there are years invested in a person, who occasionally drives you up the wall by causing drama, acting "funny" or getting in your business.

Friends usually mean well, even when their actions are questionable. Check out what friend-dilemmas these women are facing:

"My friend is married to a complete loser. I don't like her husband, and all she does is complain. I can't watch her ruin her life. Last month she called me crying, and I told her it's her choice— she can either deal with him or move on; just don't complain. Today she told me she is upset with me because I told her it's her fault she is unhappy for trying to save her marriage. That is not what I said. What should I do?"

You didn't say anything wrong, and your comments were pretty mild, especially if you don't like her husband. But if your goal is to be helpful, recognize that sometimes people just want to vent about what's going on and want someone to listen. Trying to push them to a bottom line before they're ready for change can result in them attacking you, just as your friend did. It's not because you said something bad or inaccurate, but because she needs to blame someone for her unhappiness, and you're an easier target than her spouse.

The next time your friend comes to you with relationship drama— and she will— ask her what she wants from you before you share your thoughts. If she gives you clearance to speak your mind, ask her, "What do you want to do?" Help her sort out her thoughts on whatever the problems are, and put the onus of figuring out how to solve the issue on her.

Not only is it more empowering for her to create her own solutions, but if things don't go well, she can't blame you. Once she has an answer figured out, send her back to her spouse to discuss. No matter who weighs in with insight, good or bad, it's their relationship, and only those two can solve the problems in it. You can also tell her that you are not comfortable discussing her relationship.

"A close relative is involved in a physically and verbally abusive relationship with her boyfriend. She constantly complains about him and says she wants to leave him, but she never does. I can't keep her away from him even though I have tried. (Once, when she stayed at my house and was leaving to go to his, I took her keys.) She deserves better than this and knows better. Is there any way to get through to her?"

Honestly? There's not much you can do about it. Your relative does deserve better. But as much as you want more for a loved one, you won't see any changes in her behavior until she wants it for herself.

I'd encourage you not to get involved further. She's an adult and free to make her own choices, even if that means picking a mate who is abusive and choosing to stay with him. The best thing you can do for her is to continue to support her emotionally. That's probably draining for you, but her self-esteem is extraordinarily low, and it's important that whenever, or even if, she decides that she's had enough of her volatile situation, she knows that someone has her back.

Also, since she's repeatedly mentioned ending the relationship, there is some hope that she genuinely wants out; she may just not know the best way to detach herself. The next time she complains and threatens to leave, ask her, "What would it take for you to stay away from him?" Help her become proactive by creating a plan of action. (Be forewarned: Even if, in the best-case scenario, she leaves, it does not mean she will stay gone.)

"Is it unreasonable to ask my very good friend to keep her distance as long as she is dating a married guy? Told her once how I felt about it. I do not wish to condone her behavior. Willing to resume relationship when she breaks up with the guy."

Yes. You don't need to agree with all her choices to be her friend. Surely she doesn't condone all of yours. If you don't want to hear married man escapades, then say that. But you don't go dropping real friends because they make poor relationship choices. That's not friendship, that's trying to control her.

"Do you mind your business if your friend is increasingly making reckless choices when it comes to guys that directly affect her health, employment, and finances? I feel like a bad friend by saying nothing, but I don't want her to feel like I'm judging her; I just don't want her hurt."

You can hit her with a "may I speak freely?" And express your concerns and ask her if you can help. That's a one-shot deal.

Here's the thing about adults making a mess of their lives: they know. And as much as it bothers you as a friend to watch them self-destruct, they have to want better in order for change to occur. Sometimes having attention/being "loved" is more important to them than the things you think they should value.

"I saw my friend's husband on a dating website. They have children and I don't want to disrupt their home. I'm torn. Please help. Do I tell her, and if so, how?"

In general, I'm not a fan of friends or family disclosing when they think someone in a relationship is up to activity that they shouldn't be up to. Even when you're right, there's usually no definitive proof, and the person cheating doesn't readily confess. The situation turns into a messy "he said, she said," and because there's no real confirmation, the couple stays together anyway.

Even when solid evidence exists that a partner has been unfaithful, a lot of people like to shoot the so-called messenger. The person who gets tipped off may not be willing to take action with her partner. Instead that person may look for someone to blame. The friend, who thought she was doing the right thing, often becomes the target of that person's anger and gets sidelined instead of the unfaithful partner.

In your case, take the risk of losing your friendship and disclose to your friend what you have found. You wouldn't be a very good friend if you had evidence that her husband seemed to be looking to cheat and you didn't tell her. And you don't need to be concerned about disrupting their home— that's on Husband for being on the dating website.

Don't tell your friend what you found; show her. Send her an email with a screenshot of his dating profile. A simple, "Hey, [insert friend's name], I found this on XYZ site and thought you should see" will suffice. You're a smart woman; so is she. Let her figure it out what it means.

"I have a friend who confessed to me that she slept with a mutual friend's husband. The

same mutual friend invited everyone to her house, and my friend came, acting like everything was OK. I thought it was inappropriate for her to be there and didn't speak to her other than to say "Hi" and "Bye." I do not feel comfortable watching her smile in this woman's face, and I now question if she could or would do this to me. I don't want to judge her, but I just don't feel comfortable being around her right now. Should I tell or be quiet?"

Mind your business. I imagine that the friend who told you feels guilty about her actions and needed someone to talk to. She may even be hoping that you will do her dirty work by telling the wife what her husband and the "friend" are up to. But don't make life easy for the friend or put yourself in the middle of a battle that's not yours to fight. This is for the wife, the husband and the alleged mistress to hash out whenever they get around to it.

What I don't want from you, who have no proof of the affair, is to run to your friend to say, "Guess what!" and when the wife follows up with the mutual friend and her husband about what's going on, they both adamantly deny the truth and blame you for being a messy or jealous friend. It's their word against yours. Without any proof, the wife is more than likely to go with the version of events that creates the least amount of upheaval in her life. That means you're more likely to be cut from the circle of trust than the alleged mistress or the husband.

Pull aside your cheating friend and speak to her about your discomfort with what she's told you and with being around her. Add that you don't appreciate her involving you in this drama, and encourage her to end the affair and confess to the wife about what's going on.

This is preferable to passive-aggressively offering her the silent treatment after she's confided in you. If the wife ever discovers that an affair between the mutual friend and the husband took place and that you may have known, your loyalty bases are somewhat covered.

"A friend's husband is sending me suggestive text messages (some with photos.) I'm not even leading him on, I promise. I can't even look at him in public (which is often as we run in the same circle). How do I tell her? Or should I speak with him first?"

I hate it when guys do that. Like out of all the women in the world to be inappropriate with, you gotta choose a friend of your wife's and drive a wedge between the two women? *Ugh.*

Tell him you're not comfortable with his texts and to stop contacting you. Add that if he contacts you again, you will forward his texts to his wife. It's the right thing to do, even if will be a blow to her marriage and possibly shatter the friendship between the two of you, but it's what a good friend would do. You would want someone to tell you if it was your husband, no?

"Every time my BFF gets new dick she gets flaky. I've started to make plans and cancel on her so she can get a taste of her own medicine. I know it's petty. How do I tell her that every time she gets a man she goes MIA?"

That is petty. And because people often have a hard time recognizing their behavior in other people, she probably has no clue why you're bailing on her all of the sudden.

Have a heart-to-heart chat with her. And don't go accusing. Be honest about how you feel, which is hurt that you no longer feel like a priority to her when she has a man in her life.

"One of my BFFs recently met a great guy and is head over heels. We hate it when women meet a man and then disappear on their girls, but she's doing the opposite: she always brings him when we hang out. I don't want to date him! What should I say?"

This type is more annoying than the woman who disappears. You have to tell her, "it's girl time and only ladies should come."

I never understood the dude who comes out frequently to lady-time. Like, ain't the game on? Madden didn't drop a new game? None of your boys wants to grab a beer with you? You don't need a nap? Ugh. You couldn't come up with any excuses to get out of this?

"My boyfriend feels my friends are loose. I can see why being that they have had random hook ups with his friends. It becomes an issue when we do girls' nights and he thinks something could happen. How should I handle?"

Don't neglect your girls over your man's insecurity. Your girls were there before him and might be there after him. Maybe they are "loose". Maybe not. But unless he thinks you're loose too, I don't see the problem. If you want to be petty with a point, you can tell him that you're concerned about his friends as they have hooked up with your girls.

You're not in junior high. You're not going to do whatever just because your girls do. Big girls know how to say "no" and excuse themselves when events get too turned up.

"Early on in the dating process. I would like to solidify what's going on between the two of us first before throwing him into the mix with my friends, especially when we're not official

yet. However, my friends are asking to meet him. Do you think I should bring the new guy around my friends for group dates?"

Tell your friends you'll bring him around when or if it's official. You're obviously not comfortable with the idea now, and there's no real reason that your friends need to meet him. If they like him, that's nice. If they don't, it's still nice. What matters is that you like him since you're the one that has to spend the most time with him.

"I have a lot of guy friends and we go out together a lot. Onlookers always assume that one of them is with me. How can I appear single in a group full of dudes?"

I have a lot of guy friends, and you're right, no one will approach you because you look taken. First, you have to break away from the group. And you have to be more aggressive about meeting guys. They're not going to come up because they don't want any problems with your group of guys. You have to walk up and introduce yourself and make it clear you're single.

"Is it ever ok to date the ex husband of a very good friend? I was friends with him before they met, helped through the wedding planning, was a freaking bridesmaid. Is it a no-no or just in poor taste?"

Nah, ma'am. In *A Belle in Brooklyn*, I wrote that it's ok to date *some* ex-BFs of your friends, *with permission*, of course and depending on the length of time since the break up, her current relationship status and the depth of her feelings about the relationship. In that essay, I deemed "great loves"— any guy would be described like "Big" on *Sex and the City*— entirely off-limits. It's safe to say that a husband qualifies as a great love, even if the marriage ended. To go after him would be dead wrong and your friendship would be in shambles.

My general rule about dating a friend's ex is "are you comfortable asking for permission?" If not, you shouldn't even consider it. And even if you are comfortable, things can go awry.

In my case, I did ask— not a friend, but an associate— about an ex over a dinner I'd invited her to. She said "cool", we finished our meals, then she flipped on me the next day. I didn't even know him when they dated and someone else had to tell me a couple weeks in like, "oh, you know that's XYZ's ex, right?". Me: *fugggg*. (And hence the sit down.)

They'd been broken up for 3 to 4 years. She was also living with someone at the time so she had clearly moved on. But it didn't make a difference. Folks get weird about exes, even the un-major ones. Doesn't make it right, but can make it a headache.

HIS FRIENDS

"I'm not his usual "type" and I feel his friends don't think I'm a good fit for him and don't like me. At this point (early in the relationship), they have more influence over him than I do. Could this ruin our relationship?"

They had more influence when you two were dating, not once you were in a relationship. If they don't like you now, they didn't when he was dating you either and he committed anyway. But it doesn't really matter if they like you, you're not dating them. If you're uncomfortable around them, keep the outings that involve them to a minimum. And if they are rude to you, tell your man to check them.

"My guy tells me stories about his friend's indiscretions and general attitude about commitment. This doesn't automatically make me think he's a dog or a commitment-phobe, but is it a yellow flag telling me to be cautious?"

His friends being "rolling stone" types doesn't automatically mean that he is too. Like, do you agree with your friends on everything they do?

But you should listen to his stories for his reactions to what he's telling you about. Does he think the outlook of his friend is simple or does he speak of his friend's antics with admiration? If he agrees with his friend's perspective, be careful.

"My man's best friend tried to kiss me the other night while my man went on a beer run. I always knew he liked me, but it took me by surprise. I don't want to be the chick to mess up a friendship and our relationship is very fresh. Keep it to self?"

You're not messing up the friendship, his boy did that when he tried to kiss you. If it makes you feel any better— and it probably won't— you're just a pawn to the best friend. He has some serious unresolved issues with his boy and he's using you to get to him.

You have to tell your boyfriend what happened ASAP. "Hey, the other night when you went to the store, XYZ happened while you were gone. I stopped him, [insert explanation of why you didn't say something as soon as he got back.]

As I'm responding this question, it also dawns on me how weird this scenario is. This isn't usually how men operate. There was a woman who wrote in once about a time that her brother-in-law showed up to meet his brother at the house before the brother arrived home, and the brother opted to wait in the car than come inside. Nothing was going to happen, of course, but the guy didn't want to give the appearance of something happening either. That's kinda normal for guys.

The way your scenario was supposed to play out was if his boys are at the house and he needed to make a beer run, then either the woman goes with her man or all the boys go to the store. The girlfriend is rarely left in the house with a man that's not a relative *of hers*. If you down the line, your boyfriend tries to get you to do a threesome with his best friend, remember this moment, and know you were set up by your boyfriend.

"My boyfriend has a woman friend who knows every move we make. They talk constantly, and she knows everything he does before I get an update. They grew up together and are super close. Is this just friends being friends or suspect?"

I can't give you a definitive answer based on the information given. In the best-case scenario, he hasn't adjusted to being in a relationship, or he's unaware of some of the basics that come with the "boyfriend" title. The most glaring violation is speaking about all your business, especially about your relationship, to other people. Another is that your partner is getting major news after a friend.

Let's hope for the best here. Have a conversation with boyfriend about the amount of time spent with his female friend. Ask him to set boundaries on the information he shares and pull back on the time he spends talking to her or with her. This is a reasonable request of a person in a relationship.

In the worst-case scenario, this reminds me of the classic Biz Markie song "Just a Friend," in which there's a whole lot more to the story, and it doesn't end well for you. In this situation, you're a placeholder until they can figure out how to get it right.

"My BF and his female friend abroad Skype every Thursday at a standing time. He won't miss it even if I plan something. He'll ask to plan before or after the call. He says it's their "tradition", but he and I don't have one. Why does he need tradition with a friend?"

You're keeping him company until he and this friend are in the same city. Wherever she is in the world, she takes precedence over you who is right up in his face.

The last time I heard a story similar to this, a guy was Skype-ing with the mother of child every night for years, just talking about nothing. The truth was he was still in love with her, but she had moved to another city and was in another relationship. A few days after his current (and live-in) girlfriend flipped about the nightly Skype sessions, he confessed to his ex that he wanted to be with her. She said she felt the same. Three months later, she and their child moved to his city and they got married.

So yeah, cut your losses with your dude and let him figure things out with his will-be wife.

CHAPTER FOURTEEN

Social Media Sucks

I don't advocate for social media sites, mostly because they can hurt relationships more than they can enhance them. Current divorce statistics back up my loathing. One in five divorces involves Facebook, according to a study from the American Academy of Matrimonial Lawyers.

Of course, there are couples who exist just fine on social media. The partners tend not to do much visiting to or commenting on their significant other's pages, and they definitely keep personal matters, especially quarrels, offline, where they belong. I find that couples who exercise appropriate social media boundaries to be few and far between.

Last year, BlackandMarriedwithkids.com, one of my favorite sites for relationship commentary, ran a story entitled, "My Wife Is NOT My Friend (On Facebook)." Contributing writer Eric Payne detailed the havoc wreaked on his marriage when he realized that he and his wife's status updates were, as Payne put it, "broadcast news coming straight out of our home."

Things got out of hand when the couple wasn't getting along, and the perceived-as-negative tone of their status updates elevated a passing tiff into the territory of "strong disagreement." They reached their social media tipping point when Payne questioned the motivation behind comments on his wife's photos from men he didn't know and she took offense to his sensitivity.

"It came to me late one night that there is too much out there pulling at the hearts and minds of married couples, mine included, to allow the unexpected nuances of Facebook interactions to be added to the pile," wrote Payne. "Right then and there, I knew what I had to do. I went to my wife's profile and clicked, 'Remove From Friends' without hesitation ... Now my wife and I exist as friends in the world that truly matters: the real one."

I'm obviously with Payne on this one, but many couples are not. Check out a few of their dilemmas:

"I just found out my boyfriend has a Facebook page. Of course, I investigated. He left comments like "I can't wait to kiss you" on wom-

en's pictures. And he posted pics of his ex on his wall. Should I trip?"

That he hid his page from you is one problem. That probably could have been worked out. But what he's doing on his page is even more problematic. And no wonder he hid it, given what you found on it!

Not only should you trip, you should bounce. Your boyfriend is either in another relationship or he is still on the hunt for more women.

"Would you advise people to indicate whom they are dating on FB through their relationship status? Shouldn't it be that those who really need to know about your relationship status will know or should know?"

Everybody on social media doesn't need to know who you're dating or in a relationship with. As long as people you know and care about *in the real world* know you're coupled up, that's all that matters.

Most social media pages are an assortment of actual friends, family, co-workers, classmates from the past and friends of friends. All of those people don't need to know who your boo is. When "friends" see your status change to "in a relationship with..." all they do is go to the person's page and creep thru the pictures. Humans are awful like that.

If/when you and the person don't work out and your break up or single status is announced, you invite commentary of the "what happened?" variety because you've invited people into your business by sharing it.

"I've been dating a guy for 8 months. Things are great, but he still has a picture of him and his ex together in a pic on his FB page. I never let it bother me before, figuring he would remove it when we get more serious, but he hasn't. It's been bothering me lately. Should I tell him about it?"

If you were in a relationship, you would have much more room to speak up. But you're dating. It's not "serious" if after 8 months there is still no commitment. You don't really have much leg to stand on here to ask for the picture to come down. If the ex's picture is his profile picture, you and the guy aren't ever going to evolve into more. He's still dealing with her, or at the very least hopes to get her back. He's biding his time until that happens.

"My friend thinks I am interested in a guy she used to talk to because I added him on FB and I talk to him socially. She thinks that because I said he was playing her that we should not be friendly. What should I do?"

Why would you add your friend's former boo thang? You met him through her, no? Then you shaded him so she would stop seeing him. And now you're friends? I'm with her. It seems like you're trying to holler, especially as your friend told you it bothers her and you haven't deleted him. What is so special about him that keeping him around is so important? What other reason than pushing up do you have to keep in touch with him?

If you want to go after him, say so and ask your friend's permission, as a courtesy. If you're not willing to do that, then you don't need to be "friends" with him.

"I am Facebook friends with my boyfriend. He put up a new profile picture of himself shirtless and it's pissing me off. Should I say something about it, or is this petty?"

You don't like it, say something. I'm sure he's proud of his physique and works hard for it, but he posted the pic so he could get attention from women. He's acting like a thirst-bucket right now.

Ask him to take it down. It's entirely reasonable for you not to want every woman on his page looking at his goods, and likely flirting with him because they like what they see. He would likely not be cool with a picture of you in a bikini top and your male friends lusting over you.

"I use Twitter mainly to connect with other writers and occasionally old friends. My boy-

friend is following me and constantly comments on trivial tweets because he is jealous.
Do I block him?"

If he won't stop, tell him you think it's best if you
don't follow each other anymore, then block him. Do
understand that blocking him may be the end of the
relationship. The guy who blows trivial Twitter comments out of proportion is also the guy who gets upset
when you shut him down completely.

"I've been in an on & off relationship for six
years. Recently, he asked me not to see other
people and yet, there's a female on Twitter
posting screenshots of his love texts to her.
Does it make sense for me to bring it up?"

Are you in a relationship with him? I'm unclear.

If he's not your boyfriend with title, don't cut off
anybody for him. He wants you to himself, he needs to
offer a commitment and title.

Now about this woman and her screenshots: how do
you know about her? Are you searching through his
follows and responses because you don't trust him?
And if that's the case, why are you dealing with him,
especially when after six *years* you two can't resolve
some fundamental issues (it's why you're on and off,
not just "on".)

Yes, ask about the woman. He's asking you to be
exclusive to him, you get to ask about the nature of his

relationship with the woman who seems to be flipping out over him. She sounds like a bigger problem waiting to happen.

"I was following my BF on Twitter and noticed he was getting flirty with a capital F" with a girl. When I asked him about it. He said it was nothing. How do I handle? I know I shouldn't be following him, but if there's nothing to hide..."

Set ground rules as a couple for how you two will interact with the opposite sex on Twitter and other social media. Everyone flirts to some degree, but it's not cool to do where your partner— and everyone else— can see, and document, acting up.

"It's nothing" to him. Tell him you're not cool with it and *ask* him not to do it again. Add that he wouldn't like if you did the same. If he can't stop openly flirting with other women, then he needs to be single.

"I'm very private when it comes to relationships. My boyfriend of 7 months said, "something doesn't sit right with him" (basically accusing me of cheating) because I don't want him to put me on social media and I don't put him on mine. I don't want our biz out there because I feel that it makes things go awry when people are in your business. Am I wrong?"

Not wrong. But this isn't a right/wrong scenario. It's about what works for you and him as a couple. Right now he feels he's being hidden. He wants it known that you are not available to date. Can you mention each other by your initials or a pet name in captions or status updates every once in awhile? Can you make a game out of featuring each other in pictures where the other person can be acknowledged, but not really seen? I'm thinking pictures of hand-holding or shared dinner plates or pictures from a distance.

I'm with you. I don't think acknowledging each other on social media is all that important to a relationship. But Boyfriend does and his feelings have to be considered. If you're not willing to budge, you may end up without a relationship as he thinks you're cheating. Only you can determine if it's better to be alone with your privacy or with him and semi-exposed.

"I've noticed that my fiancé follows numerous big booty models and twerk videos on Instagram. I try so hard to not let this bother me, but I can't help but feel a twinge of jealously when he likes a post. I don't have a big butt, but I do consider my shape to be really nice. I never considered myself an insecure person. I mentioned it to him and he said, "it's no big deal. She's pretty and I have no chance of meeting her." Should I just have kept my feelings to myself?"

No. It's good that you have open lines of communication with your mate. You said how you feel and he assured you that it was nothing.

Men like to look at ass. There is nothing you can do to stop this. And because he likes big ass he has no chance with, doesn't mean he also doesn't like your ass too. But he is crossing the line by "liking" the pictures. It's the online equivalent of telling a woman that he thinks she's hot.

Tell him he can look all day— because it's not like you can stop him— but you would prefer if he didn't like the pictures. Hopefully, he'll abide by your wishes. Either way, stop stalking his page to see what activity he is up to. You are driving yourself into insecurity

CHAPTER FIFTEEN

Fix it, Jesus

I was raised in the church, but I'm not exactly what you would call a religious person, or not in the traditional sense. I only go to church when I am out of town (which is actually quite a lot), but I have an all-day running dialogue with God, some of it out-loud.

While I may not be present for most altar calls, I recognize the religion plays a profound role in many women's lives— 74 percent of Black women described living a religious life as ""very important" in a 2012 poll conducted by The Washington Post and the Kaiser Family Foundation— which, of course, includes their romantic relationships. I may not be an expert on

Biblical teachings, but I am in communication and bottom-lining what matters (or not).

Check out the conflicts these women faced when their walk with God intersected with their love lives:

"My BF complains that I won't go to church with him. My Mom, who is a big church-goer, wants me to give in. She says he is a nice man with a good family and a good job in the family business. I had a bad experience growing up in the church and I don't want to return. Should I end it?"

Your relationship with God and church is a personal one, and should not be dictated by your boyfriend or your mother, who each are not respecting your decision. It's disturbing that your mother seems more concerned about your boyfriend's "status" than she is about whatever happened to you in church.

If you don't want to go to church, then don't. Explain to your boyfriend what your hesitation is about so he understands the backstory and doesn't think you're being difficult. If he's not willing to respect your wishes, then you may need to consider leaving the relationship.

"I am engaged to a great guy. He has a great career, goals and truly loves me! One issue: GOD! I've asked him to attend church with me

and he finds excuses not to attend! Sometimes, I feel this is a deal breaker. We are supposed to get married soon. Am I being petty?"

He doesn't want to go. That's why after 4 years he hasn't. Instead of asking him to go, ask him why he doesn't and what it would take for him to go. A lot of men don't attend church (which is why in many churches so many women fill the pews). The reasons men give for not going to church are they don't trust the ministers, it seems like a lot of hoopla, and they don't get much of the experience. If you want your man to go, you may have to find a church together where he is comfortable. He also may not be big on God so there's nothing to compel him.

If you're heavily into church, and want a partner who is as well, he's not it. The hardcore Christian folks will tell you that a man who doesn't attend/have a strong relationship with God isn't the right man. And he's not going to miraculously change after the wedding. If you can't accept that he doesn't go to church, then do NOT marry him.

"What do you think about two people getting married where one is a Christian and the other is saved and believes in God but is unsure about religion and going to church?"

Depends on how heavy the Christian partner is into church and what he his/her expectations are of his/her

partner. That and whether or not the Christian partner respects the laid-back attitude about religion ex-
hibited by the other person. If the arrangement has
worked throughout the courtship, it should be fine. If
one of the partners expects the other's outlook to
change after the wedding, that's a huge problem.

**"Has someone ever broken up with you be-
cause of your faith? This recently happened to
me and I'm rather confused, but ultimately I
know it's for the best because faith is a very
important to me in a potential partner."**

Eh... I dated guy who was pretty into church. He
wanted us to go every Sunday and to "expand" on my
prayers when I blessed the food. Once he pulled over
on the side of the road after an argument and insisted
we pray.

We broke up for a different reason, but I'm sure my
relaxed attitude toward religion played a factor in the
demise of the relationship. (Random: he called me two
years after we broke up to apologize. He doesn't even
go to church anymore. Or pray. No clue what happened.)

That said, you solely get to determine what is important to you, so if a partner with faith is what you
want, then you shouldn't settle for less (it won't make
you happy anyway.)

"In relationship and discussing marriage. Parents are against me even dating him based off of the fact his religion differs from ours. Religion is important to me but not a deal breaker. I highly respect my family's opinions. Mom has gone to the extreme and isn't speaking to me. I'm not sure what to do."

If you want to get married— or not— do it because it's right for you. Not to rebel and not because you're trying to make others happy.

You're an adult. You get to act like one. And that means deciding what is a deal breaker for you— or not It's YOUR life. Respecting the opinions of your parents does not mean doing whatever they say.

Your mother is exhibiting control issues. She's having the adult equivalent of a tantrum because you won't give her, her way. Make the decision that is right for YOU whether she's speaking to you or not. And just so you know, you give in on this one because she won't talk to you, and she will pull this move every time she doesn't approve of your decision.

CHAPTER SIXTEEN

"It's Not You, It's Me"

Years ago, I was dating a lovely older man who adored me. I enjoyed being with him because he was funny, kind and thoughtful. At one point I did see a future with him, but I was more caught up in what I thought I was *supposed to do*— get married— than what I really *wanted* to do. I wasn't quite sure what that was, but it wasn't getting married.

For the first year or so, we didn't have "forever talks." We just sort of hung out and enjoyed each other. Around the 18-month mark, when he started talking about a future together, I kept my mouth shut about what I could foresee— or not. I told myself that it was all talk, that it didn't mean anything, really, if there was no ring, or that if he really wanted to know, he'd ask and not assume.

The truth was, I had a good thing; and when I had to do more to keep it, I wasn't on board. There's no way around it: I was using him. Admittedly, it was childish. At 24, I was barely grown and selfish, which can't be excused at any age.

I finally told him what I really thought one evening after we'd spent the day talking about the guest list for our wedding. It wasn't easy, but if I'd dragged it out any further, I probably would have been confessing at the altar.

He yelled at me (for the first time) and scared the crap out of me. Then he yelled some more because he was offended that after all the time we'd spent together, I seemed scared that he would hurt me. That memory dulls in comparison to the look on his face when he left my apartment for the last time.

Break ups are never easy, but often necessary, if for no other reason than to clear the path for someone new. Here are a few women facing break up dilemmas:

"How do you feel about couples taking a break? My man suggested it, but I don't know how I feel about people being able to check in

and out of a relationship when they feel like it. Does it say something about my self respect if I let him take a break?"

Taking a break isn't an indictment of your self-respect, but it does indicate that there are some glaring issues in your relationship that you may be overlooking. The most obvious concern is poor communication. You and your guy seem to be facing an unnamed conflict that you aren't able to resolve. The suggestion of a break is the result of ongoing frustration and an attempt to avoid a glaring issue.

Here's one of the problems with breaks: they often make the problems worse. The idea is that you take some space to clear your head. You're not focused on solving the issues anymore, you're focused on getting freedom from a situation that's been bogging you down for weeks or months or even years. Problems don't get solved by avoiding them.

The other glaring issue here is that there are no real rules for breaks. You're technically single, but there's the idea that you'll "work it out" someday so you're not supposed to really behave like a single person. See how ridiculous (and grey) that sounds?

Instead of agreeing to a break, tell your partner that you want to re-focus on tackling the issues that are shaking up your relationship. What is it that he wants? What do you want? And what creative ways can you compromise to make each other happy? If you can't find a solution that works for you both, agree to disagree or actually break up and go your separate ways.

I'm clearly no fan of breaks, but if you agree to one, set ground rules with your partner that include how long the break will last and what's permissible behavior— or not— during your time apart.

"Currently in a break situation for about three weeks. Boyfriend requested it because we weren't in a good place. I learned he's been spending time with a girl I'd always suspected he was attracted to. I'm heartbroken and confused. Should I address it, and if so, how?"

He's keeping you on hold while he figures out exactly what he wants to do with the new woman. And he's not technically in a relationship since he's on "break" so he's not doing anything wrong. And you can't say much about it with any ground to stand on because you aren't really together.

If you don't want to put up with this, don't. Call him and tell him the break and the relationship are over as him dating someone else isn't what you signed up for.

"You say people shouldn't take breaks to work on themselves, then get back together, that they should work issues out while together. But you broke up with CBW for 5 months and

now you're engaged. Several married couples I know broke up for months or years with their now-husband/wife. Are you wrong on this one, Belle?"

The five months you refer to was neither a break nor a break up. We dated. He didn't want what I wanted, so I bailed. We weren't in a relationship, so there was nothing to break from.

There's a difference between "break"' and "break up". Breaking is messy because it's a grey area and the parameters aren't clear. You're technically single, expected to act like you're in a relationship and there's usually no determined time period for the separation. It's a mess waiting to happen.

If it ain't working and you need to break *up*— as in everyone is free, so be it. Breaking up is also not a communication or solution-to-problem strategy. When you leave, expect to stay gone. There's no exit, and hoping to get back together. If it happens, so be it.

"Not [original poster], but in same situation. I also "wanted something different than him." My guy has reached out, but wanna protect my heart. Can't be just friends. When you went through this with CBW, did you speak over the 5 months or did you remain distant until he stepped up?"

He called from time to time to ask how I was. I actually started dating someone else and was in a relationship (disaster decision).

CBW called once after I did a Fox 5 TV segment and mentioned I had a boyfriend on live TV. He hit me before I left the news station like, "you got a man now?!"

On his birthday, he called to ask if I could spend it with him. My answer: "no." I went out with my dude at the time... and actually ran into CBW's boys at a restaurant. *Awkward.* I left with my dude. The guy already felt a way about me mentioning CBW so often and I didn't want them to meet. (CBW looked similar except he was taller, browner, broader and with Brooklyn swag.)

Short version: dude broke up with me. I was a mess because I'd been unceremoniously rejected twice back-to-back and was on my "what is wrong with me?" trip.

My "wife" called CBW and told him I was single again. He showed up that night, and stuck around for weeks under the guise of "I just wanna make sure you're OK." When I felt better, I told him, "I can't jump from one bad situation to the next. I like you, *a lot*, but you're not offering anything. I respect that... but no."

He told me, "OK", then he dipped for 2 to 3 weeks. He called one day, asking to see me. I told him I was good and wasn't going down that road again. He said he wanted to start over, get to know me again, and he wanted a relationship if things went well. For the next month, he acted like a man on a mission: consistently on point, interested, and happily willing to be inconvenienced.

Four to 5 weeks later— I should have made him wait longer— he asked me to be his lady.

"Do you owe an ex or soon to be ex, an explanation of why you don't want to be in the relationship anymore? What if you just don't want to be. It's not some big reason. I just don't want to be in one."

Technically, you don't have to tell anyone the reason you don't want to stick around. "I don't want to do this anymore" is a sufficient answer. However, having been on the receiving end of that speech, I know that the lack of a reason hurts like hell. Only be vague if you've been done wrong, and really want to stick it to someone when you go. Otherwise, give a reason, even it's "I just want to be single is all." It's the evolved equivalent of "It's not you, it's me". But it's better than nothing at all.

"BF of 2.5 years disappeared on me at the beginning of the year. He completely ignored my attempts to contact him for weeks so I decided to move on. I am still hurt and confused. Is

this a common way for a dude to end a relationship? How do I move on without closure?"

Falling off the face of the earth is singlehandedly
the worst way to break up with someone. I was in a
relationship with someone once, and he was supposed
to visit me for Thanksgiving. He called to say he was
on his way, then just never showed up. He texted me
days later (after ignoring me for several days) to say he
had changed his mind, and if I wanted to talk about it,
I could call him.

It's not a common break up, but it does happen. It's
the exit method for people who don't have the back-
bone to say, "it's over." Just going quietly into the
night is their way of avoiding drama and conflict for
themselves, ignoring that the approach wreaks havoc
on a person that he once cared about, or pretended he
did.

The good news here is that there is more than one
kind of closure. There's the wrap-up conversation that
everyone desires, but you can also get closure thru:

Forgiveness: I once heard someone describe being
angry with someone who doesn't know or doesn't care
being the equivalent of drinking poison and expecting
someone else to die.

You have every right to be angry with your ex, but
your anger doesn't solve anything, and only hurts you.
So forgive, not for him, *but for you.* The anger para-
lyzes you in your ugliest moment and ties you to the

person who rejected you. Forgiveness loosens the hold he still has on you.

Write it Out: Get the thoughts out of your head and onto paper, or the screen. Putting your story into words will help you see the relationship clearly, including some red flags you may have missed about your partner. Once you've documented your story and your truths, you won't feel the need to incessantly replay the story in your head.

Create Your Own Ending: Choose your own end date for the relationship and mark it on the calendar. On the day, treat yourself to something special to mark the new beginning in your life.

"What is a respectable amount of time to start dating after a break up?"

Technically, you're in the clear to date the day after a relationship ends. You're no longer committed so there's no longer a need to be exclusive or consider your ex.

You're probably better off waiting about 30 days, minimum. Many of us make a habit of bouncing from one partner to the next out of fear of being alone with our own thoughts. You're best served to spend some time with you, figuring out what went wrong in the relationship and the role you played in the demise.

Also, because so many women tend to lose themselves in relationships, it's nice to take a breather and re-discover who you are as just you, and not "XYZ's girlfriend".

"Doesn't dating the day after a break up look bad and won't your ex flip? That actually happened to me. I went on a date and ex saw me, called me up and accused me of knowing the guy while we were together. He also bad mouthed me to his friends. It was horrible. How do you prevent the fall out of dating too soon?"

Your ex wasn't over you, and he was going to bad mouth you no matter what you did or didn't do, good or bad. There's a type of person who does that when they feel rejected. You aren't the problem. He is. You don't owe your ex anything once the relationship is over. Because he was jealous and acted out doesn't mean you should tread lightly to appease his fragile ego. You're not together anymore, you don't have to be exclusive.

Go on and live your life. Let people talk. They will do it no matter what you do. Don't let yourself be held hostage to that.

"What is the rule of thumb on dating during the divorce process? Do men expect a divorce to be final in order to take a woman seriously? Is it unfair or wrong to show an interest in

other men while you are waiting for the final decree?"

Don't date until your divorce is final. That outlook may seem strict, especially for people who live in, say, North Carolina, which requires one year of separation before allowing a couple to file for even a no-fault divorce; Connecticut, which requires an 18-month waiting period before allowing a couple to file; or even Maryland, which requires a one-year wait. That can seem like a long time to "move on," especially when you are 100 percent positive that you and your spouse won't reunite. I'd encourage you to use the time between your separation and your divorce to heal emotionally from your marriage.

Since you're looking to be taken "seriously" by men, that means you're not dating just for kicks, and you might want to marry again. You should know that two-thirds of second marriages fail, according to psychiatrist Mark Banschick, author of *The Intelligent Divorce*. That's not to discourage you from believing in a second chance at love; it's to warn you not to rush into anything "serious" too soon. It's imperative that you take this time to do a personal assessment of yourself and what led to the demise of your marriage so that you don't repeat those mistakes.

You are worried about what a potential dating partner may feel, but you should also want to keep in mind how your still-current *spouse* may react to you exploring new options now. Dating before the divorce is final may upset your otherwise reasonable future ex and make him (more) unreasonable while you're trying to negotiate custody arrangements or the division of assets.

Your desire for companionship at this particular time could cost you a lot— literally and figuratively. Try to sit still a while longer. Let your desire to move on motivate you to wrap up your marriage quickly by focusing on what's really important in the divorce negotiations.

"My boyfriend and I were together for just shy of three years. It's been months and I can't get over him. We were talking marriage and kids. It feels like a piece of me is missing even though I know I'm a whole person. I feel like I'm wandering through life right now. How do you get over love?"

If you've given yourself time to get over your ex, it's imperative that you take *more time* since you haven't *yet* reached your goal.

Many women who find themselves stuck in a rut are there because they've placed an extreme premium on being in a relationship and misinterpret a breakup as a sign of a personal shortcoming on their part. Instead of thinking of ways to move on, they dwell on all the things they could have done differently or daydream about how to get their ex back in the fold. Other women who just can't seem to let go often have placed their former partner on a pedestal and believe that the experiences and feelings they had in the relationship can't be duplicated anywhere else.

Those are normal feelings just after a breakup, but if you've been feeling them for so long that even you think it's been too long, it's time to stop harping and start healing— now. Start by accepting that your relationship status does not determine your worth. It is better, in all cases, to be single than to be in a dysfunctional partnership. Once you've got that part down, analyze why your relationship went wrong and what role(s) you each played in its demise. Accept responsibility for your shortcomings and create takeaways to do better in your future relationships. Finally, forgive yourself and your partner for both of your mistakes.

None of these steps are simple and accomplishing them does not happen overnight. Just as if there were physical damage to your body, a broken heart needs time to heal. It is imperative that you allow yourself a chance to recover properly if you want to have successful relationships in the future.

Last but not least, pour all that love that you were giving to your ex into yourself. All those kind words and compliments, the attention to detail, the desire to make him happy? Do that for you now to build yourself back up.

"I have a great guy. He listens, is *sooo* supportive and honest and has a solid career. He keeps me laughing and the sex is amazing. But I still compare this relationship to that with my first love (who treated me terribly) and sadly it just doesn't top it. How do you know when a guy is The One?"

Don't be like Jill Scott's husband in "Why Did I Get Married?" and throw away a person who has 80 percent of what you want just to have the other 20. No one is perfect, but your question seems less about knowing when a guy is "the one" and more about being attracted to dysfunction. You're telling me you have a great guy who treats you well, but you're pining for a man who treated you "terribly." Healthy relationships don't really have a lot of drama, but terrible ones have plenty. So maybe you're missing the emotional rollercoaster, or maybe you were used to having to go above and beyond to prove yourself to someone. sWhen you have a guy who just loves on you just because you're you, it doesn't feel genuine or earned.

It sounds like the issue here isn't your man, or your ex, but you. You're not accustomed to being in a healthy relationship, and you have negative feelings about your worthiness or "loveable"-ness, so you're unwittingly sabotaging a healthy situation to make it more familiar, i.e., dysfunctional. You are going to have to change the way you think about yourself, and men, and relationships before you're ready to be in a healthy one. The first step is learning to act in your own best interest and choosing men who treat you well over those who don't.

"My ex portrays himself as this great guy, but I know things about him that would shock people, especially his new girlfriend. I've spent months going back and forth between thinking he deserves revenge and others should know the truth, and thinking 'he's not worth it, move on'. How do you feel about getting revenge on the ex that hurt you? Nothing involving harm to the person or property— just to expose him for what he is."

You think you have some sort of upper hand because you have information about him that you think could ruin his reputation. What you don't realize is that you've already given him the upper hand by spending months of your life still dwelling on him. You're still hurt. I get it. But you have to let it go.

Here's what will happen if you spill your ex's tea. Your friends and his friends will listen, and they will laugh and they will call others and retell your tales. They'll also wonder why, if what you say is true, you stayed with him. Then they'll wonder why, all this time later, you're running your mouth about the past. They'll ask each other why you are still so hung up on a guy who, by your own account, was so awful. (That's also a question you should ask yourself.)

Your ex will get over it quickly. He has a new woman and she's not leaving him. Add to that, all the information you have is about the past, not the present. Even if what you say is true, it's months-old info.

Forgive him. While he's enjoying life with the next woman, you have yet to meet anyone to treat you the way you deserve because you're holding on to so much animosity about your past. Your bitterness is going to block your blessings.

"My ex and I have mutual friends, and I've learned that he is slandering my name. Is it worth addressing and defending myself. I'm surprised some people are siding with him. What do I do?"

It's only worth addressing *with him*. You don't need to defend yourself to other people, who really who don't care anyway. This is just amusing gossip to them. The people who side with him weren't all that fond of you anyway. Be thankful you now know who your real friends and enemies are.

He's not happy about the break up, and he's telling his side, perhaps with some embellishment, for revenge. Call him and tell him what you heard. Be the bigger person— as a strategy— and tell him you're disappointed to hear the things that he is saying and ask if there's anything he needs to get off his chest with you. Giving him the attention he so obviously seeks, may quiet him down.

WHEN HE MOVES ON

When I do interviews about my career, sometimes people ask what my professional turning point was, that moment when everything came together. I remember the date, but it's not because it was my first time as an expert on a TV show. The same day I taped VH1s *Let's Talk About Pep* was also the same day that my "ex", who I hadn't spoken to in almost a year, started blowing up my phone.

I was mad at him about something or another, but I was always getting mad at him and we were always back and forth. I guess in the back of my mind, I figured we'd work on us again someday, but currently, I wasn't willing to put forth the effort. I was focused on my career.

But he called while I was getting my TV make-up done, and I sent him to voicemail. I didn't want any distractions before I went on set. I knew something was up when he called again as I was headed to shoot at a new location. I ignored him again. After a 12-hour day, I called him back when I was headed home in a cab. I braced myself for the worst: he was dying, he was married, someone was pregnant.

Sigh. She was pregnant. She was due in about a month. He wanted to tell me in person, but...

I cut him off: "Congratulations. I'll call you back, OK?"

I cried the whole way home, the whole night and called out of work the next day. My mother came up for the weekend to console me. That's how bad I took it.

Somehow I missed that an ex moving on *forreal, forreal* was "a thing" before it happened to me. So when these ladies wrote in, even knowing it was a wee bit irrational, I was all in their feelings with them.

"I found out this morning that my ex has a new girlfriend. I feel just awful. He was my first love. What should I do to get past this?"

I tell you what you shouldn't do: call. Stay off his *and her* social media profiles too. You will never feel better about yourself wondering, "but why wasn't it me?", or incessantly looking at pictures of him looking happy with someone else, or comparing yourself to another woman.

When you broke up, you stuffed down your feelings, you didn't do the hard work of getting over your ex, which is why you're taking this revelation hard. You put off what Iyanla Vanzant likes to call "your work", so you're going to have to do it on the back end. Figure out what your ex has that for whatever reason, you don't think you can find elsewhere. (If you did, you wouldn't be holding on to him.) Pinpoint that trait or set of traits, and find them in a person who can build a healthy relationship with. It sounds easier than it is. It takes awhile.

"My ex is considerably younger than me. It was a brief fling, but I admired his potential. When I grew bored of our relationship, I sent a sweet goodbye text message and moved on. He's now dating a girl his age who is the epitome of crass. I want to warn him but I can't decide if I'm truly concerned or simply jealous."

This is all ego. You don't care. If you did, you would not have discarded him carelessly with a text when you were "bored" with him.

He's a person, not a play-thing. And you sound salty that he has moved on and with a woman who is considerably younger than you. Whether she is crass or not is not your concern, nor is the younger man you used and discarded when he was no longer amusing to you.

"Ran into former Friend with Benefits. We still flirt hard through texts even now that sex has ended. He was with fiancée. (I was super surprised he was engaged.) The girl was super rude to me, giving nasty looks. Am I wrong for wanting to call him and give him a piece of my mind?"

You have no moral high ground here. You're carrying on with an engaged man and you're mad his fiancée was rude to you? Ma'am! You got what you deserved here, even if she doesn't know what going on. (Her spidey senses may have said something was up or better, she probably heard his version of events with you, which weren't flattering.)

No matter what she did, you're way out of your lane to call him about how his fiancée acted. You're way down on the hierarchy scale from her. You think he's going to go to his fiancée and chat with her about how she spoke to the woman he's low key creeping with? Come now.

Let's cut to the chase here: you felt "a way" about him being engaged, especially since you text with him regularly and he didn't deem you important enough to mention to you that he's getting married. You're a little salty, so in retaliation you want to be a little messy. I get it, but don't do it. How about you just don't text him anymore and call it square?

"My ex recently got married. I'm extremely hurt because they only dated for a year before he proposed. Just six months before he met her, he and I were still trying to work it out. I called and demanded answers and he basically

just held the phone. How does a guy go from one relationship to the next with such ease?"

It doesn't sound like he went to one relationship to the other "with ease". By your own timeline, there were about 18 months between when he was last dealing with you and a proposal to her. And being as he just got married, that's another minimum six months added on between proposal and wedding. That means it's been at least two years between trying to make things work with you and marrying someone else. That's not all that fast.

To pick up the phone and demand answers of a man with a wife like he owed you anything? You were way out of line there. His timeline and his marriage aren't the problem here. It's your inability to move on.

"I have an acute disdain for my verbally abusive, manipulative ex. He stopped speaking to me (how we broke up) and 2 months later he was involved and eventually engaged to an associate of mine. Will see him at a function soon. I don't want to even see or acknowledge him, but I'm hurt. He owes me an apology."

You are walking around mad about a man who doesn't know or care. The only person you're hurting is you.

He doesn't owe you anything and even if he did, what you're owed and what you are likely to get would be two different things. If it makes you feel any better, the next chick is getting the exact same treatment you got. He didn't leave and become a model boyfriend. Be thankful he walked out of your life. You should have kicked him out. That you aren't putting up with that sh-- anymore is a blessing. Be thankful, not bitter.

"I want my ex to be happy for me and say I deserve true love and a man who will love me unconditionally. He didn't say it and that hurts. Am I expecting too much?"

Yes, entirely. You're giving your ex too much power to define your life that he does not deserve or even have. It would be nice if it said it, but him saying it doesn't make it true (or false, or anything, really) and it's not his job to make you feel complete, not as your ex, and not as your man. That's YOUR job. And while it might be great closure to hear him wish you well, it's not even necessary for him, a mere mortal, to say.

Him saying it doesn't make it any more true than if you said it to yourself, so YOU say it to you since you have power to create the life you want for yourself: "I deserve true love and a man who will love me unconditionally." Go on and add, "I have not found it *yet, but I will.*"

CHAPTER SEVENTEEN

The Ex Factor

Twenty percent of the dating and relationship questions I've answered are some form of "Do you think I
should give my ex a second chance?" Especially around
the holidays, people get to thinking about how their ex
fit right in with the family at Thanksgiving, the
thoughtful present on Christmas, or the New Year's
Eve celebration when you wondered, "Is this 'the
One'?"

I find the appeal of an ex isn't so much about having
genuine feelings for the actual person, but more about
not wanting to put forth the effort to find someone
who is a better match. Looking for love requires effort
and risk. So often, getting that old thing back means

heading down a road with familiar curves and forgetting that path already led to a dead end.

Your ex might someday have a change of heart (or not). But either way, you shouldn't wait around for it to occur. Go ahead and live your life, and if the ex shows up as a changed person *with actions* to back up his (or her) words, then hear him (or her) out if you've somehow managed not to get otherwise occupied in the meantime.

When this happens, go slow. A lot of people make the mistake of jumping right back into the thick of the relationship because there are memories and shared history that make the situation comfortable. They forget that something occurred that led one of you to sum up the other person, evaluate that person's overall worth and decide, "I can do better or bad on my own."

Unfortunately, there's no clear-cut answer to whether it's worth being friends or trying again. Making the "right" decision depends on why the relationship ended. If there was an issue that you just couldn't hash out then— communication, misplaced priorities or money woes— but, with clearer heads and hopefully some maturity, it can be addressed now, then reconsidering an ex could be worth *a discussion*. If you were treated poorly— any form of abuse, infidelity or you couldn't trust him— then don't give another chance, no matter how much your partner claims to have changed. What's equally important to think about while you contemplate what to do about an ex is what both of you are willing to do differently this time so you don't repeat the mistakes of your past. If you don't change, or better, improve, you will only break up again, likely for the same reasons. And that's just more drama for everyone.

"When breaking up with someone, do you suggest a clean break with no contact or is it okay to keep in touch sparingly as long as no intimate boundaries are crossed? It wasn't just a bad break up and feeling exist on both ends."

I suggest no contact. It's the equivalent of ripping the Band-Aid off and facing the sharp pain versus the dull pain of peeling the bandage away slowly. It's very hard to get over someone when you have lingering feelings and are interacting with one another. The lingering feelings also block you from moving on because you're emotionally caught up.

Once you both take some time *apart* to heal from the relationship, you have a better chance of actually being friends in the long run.

"My ex and I remained friends after our break up. He has a girlfriend now, but he's constantly telling me he wants to be with me and the only reason he's with her is because we're not together. I think he told me he's thinking

about marrying her to get a reaction from me. How do I get him to see I'm fine with being friends?"

You're not friends with your ex. A friend doesn't "constantly" tell you that he wants to be in a relationship with you even when you're both single, and especially not when he's in a relationship. Friends also don't ignore your boundaries. You've said "no" several times and he continues to push up despite you trying to shut him down.

But this uncomfortable situation isn't all on him. You're participating in this by continuing to engage him and you need to take accountability for that as well. You're saying "no", but every time you've answered the phone or responded to a text after he's pushed up, your actions are saying, "well, maybe." He keeps approaching because he's going by what you do, not what you say.

Let's keep it 300: one of the reasons you continue to speak to him despite protesting the attention is because it's flattering. Who doesn't like to hear "I miss you" from someone they cared for? You don't want him, but you want him to want you. That's all ego and you shouldn't let it get the best of you, or continue to fuel this drama, because really, that's what this is. This ends when you stop fanning this clichéd flame.

"Is it wrong to cut an ex out of your life completely and make sure they can no longer contact you?"

You're not obligated to keep anyone in your life that you don't want there. But completely eliminating someone that you cared for deeply should be reserved for the people that did you dirty. If you didn't get dragged during the relationship or on the way out, it's fine not to block an ex from your life. If you were treated poorly, however? *Delete. Delete. Delete.*

"I've been trying to maintain a friendship with my ex who broke up with me, but he continuously harps on new people I'm dating. It's borderline harassment. He's a great friend, but it's OD stressful. What to do?"

You're exes, not friends. If you were, he wouldn't care who you dated, and certainly would not harp on it.

Be careful not to mistake his seeming jealously for interest. He doesn't want you to move on and he wants you to be into him, but that's not interest, that's ego. If he were interested, he would be trying to get back with you.

"I broke up with my ex over his lying and he's never really apologized for it. He reaches out to me occasionally like nothing is wrong.

It's infuriating and I want to address it, but also don't want to seem like I care. Should I just speak my piece once and be done or ignore him?"

Why do you continue to communicate with someone who treated you poorly in the relationship now that it's over? If he couldn't be a good boyfriend to you, he's not going to be any better— or more honest— as a friend. And on top of that, he hasn't acknowledged that he was wrong or apologized.

You want to pretend you don't care, but you do, and a lot if you're "infuriated". Stop hiding your feelings. Say whatever it is you need to say to him to feel like you've stood up for yourself, and then please, stop answering the phone.

"On a marathon phone convo with a new guy. Old guy beeps in at 1:30 AM. I answered, then went back to new guy. I haven't heard from him in two weeks. In hindsight, I realize I shouldn't have answered the call, I know. But was that enough to phase me out? Was I wrong?"

You need to set boundaries with your ex, the most obvious being the times he calls your phone. He's no longer your man and the loss of title and relationship should come with a loss of access as well.

By clicking over at that time of night, it showed the new guy that there's someone else in the picture who has a lot of access to you, and that guy takes precedence over him. Your lack of boundaries with the ex is blocking your potential blessings for the future, as evidenced by the new guy losing interest. And yes, it was enough to phase you out— obviously.

"BF has an issue with me being friends with a guy I hooked up with in college... 16 years ago. Now he needs to "rethink the relationship". We are all adults so I don't see what the issue is here. People can't be friends with exes?"

People can be friends with exes *eventually*. Your guy sounds incredibly insecure to consider breaking up with you over someone you made out with a decade and a half ago. That, or he was looking for an excuse to leave the relationship. Or he's using the implication of a break up to manipulate you into giving him his way.

Proper protocol dictates that if someone comes between you and your mate, then that person has to go. That you've seemingly chosen to hang on to an old friend instead of your man indicates there's more to the friendship or you're not really all that into your man. Given his reaction when he doesn't get his way, I get why.

Take that Old Thing Back?

"Recently my ex emailed me (I've blocked him from calling or messaging me). He wants to try the relationship again. We were together one-and-a-half years. I don't know what to make of it. It threw me off. Is it ever OK to go back to an ex?"

Before a former couple considers reuniting, they need to have a few candid discussions on the front end— that means before they are back together— about what went wrong and how the previous issues can be addressed and resolved. They should also begin to re-date each other almost as if they've met for the first time. Exes who return don't immediately regain all-access and full benefits of a relationship.

You haven't said exactly why your relationship ended, but whatever happened during or after the breakup was enough for you to block him from calling or texting you. That's not a normal reaction to a breakup. Usually when people tell me they've gone to that extent, it's because the person 1) did them really wrong in the end, 2) was making harassing or threatening contact or 3) would not take "It's over" for an answer. This is not the type of person you should consider going back to.

It's also notable to me that you point out that he wants to work things out, but you don't express the same desire. I get a lot of queries about exes, and most often there's a line or two that says, "I miss him" or "I still love him" but "I don't know what to do." You haven't done that. Your letter is about what he wants and then the length of time you were together, and that's not enough reason to go back to someone.

"I've been thinking a lot about my ex lately. Do you believe there can ever be a point where exes have truly changed their ways, can really prove themselves and live happily ever after with the people they once treated poorly?"

Not likely. People can change, of course, but unless there's some life-altering event like a religious conversion, kicking an addiction or getting over a serious illness, your ex isn't likely to have a complete change of heart. If the breakup and the aftermath didn't result in an "aha moment" that made that person realize he or she had been taking you for granted, your ex is unlikely to do a 180-degree conversion months or years later and become the person you always envisioned he or she would be. That's most likely to happen on TV.

"My ex asked me to get back together. I'm so over him. After I told him "no", he got angry and demanded to know why I won't reconsider. I'm tired of saying the same thing over and over. What else can I say or do to get across that I'm done? He won't go away."

He feels quite entitled to having his way, and I'm guessing that sense of entitlement had something to do with why the relationship ended. He's annoying, not respecting your boundaries and you clearly don't want to be bothered. There's no talking to him further. Block him, and call it a life.

"Ex and I still have sex. We both agreed that we may want to get back together in the future and I feel I may want that more than him. He was a good boyfriend, but he cheated. I forgave him. It's fun now. But how do I protect my heart?"

Stop having sex with him. Some women may be able to have sex with no emotional attachment, but you are not that woman. You have feelings for him, and if he said "let's do this again" tomorrow— which he won't— you would be all over it. He's just having sex. You are settling for a piece of the whole man because that's all he's offering.

In your head, you're keeping him around and keeping him interested. But that's not how he sees it. He used to have to make a commitment and do boyfriend duties for access to sex. Now he gets the benefits without any of the headaches. What's the incentive to be your man again?

Acknowledgements

Thank you to my parents for being my first example of a relationship and showing me up close and personal what it takes to make a marriage last (for 38 years and counting.) Thank you, Dad, for checking in daily about the progress of this book. (I apologize for being short when I was on deadline.) And thank you, Mum, once again, for teaching me how to read and leaving *Waiting to Exhale* on the counter that morning.

CBW: Thank you. For everything. I got on the subway one morning, not knowing that ride would change my life. I was going fast on my own, you showed me how to go far. Thank you for holding my hand on the Second Act of this wild, weird, unpredictable journey that is our life.

Jess, Kev, Kedda, Toya, Parler, Nicole, Rich, Briana, and Johnica (and all my other friends), thank you for understanding while I went AWOL to write (and re-write) this book, both versions, and for always being available to chat and hang out when I (briefly) came up for air. To Mack: thank you for dealing with my last-minute demands to format the book cover, *and* design the invites to the launch parties *and* then shooting the parties too. (Someday, I will remember the batteries.)

To my manager, Andrea Wade, my publicists Christina Rice and Tiffany Moten, and my attorney Amy Goldson: thank you for doing your official duties with such expertise so I can focus on creating. And for believing in and supporting this evolving thing we call "Brand Belle". A special thank you for adding therapist to your job descriptions and never complaining about the extra duty.

Thank you to my work-family at *The Root*, especially Donna Byrd, Lyne Pitts and Genetta Adams. I've missed more deadlines than I count working on this book. Thank you for your patience though this exhausting process.

To the Belleionaires: Eight years and counting. BOOM! We did it again! Thank you for continuously believing in me.

CPSIA information can be obtained at www.ICGtesting.com
Printed in the USA
LVOW11s1755171214

419284LV00007B/976/P

9 780990 819400